CENTRAL ASIA PHYSICAL

Our approximate routes ⎯⎯⎯

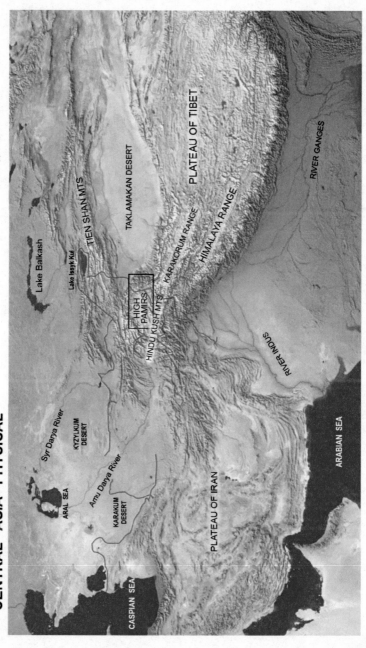

For Telly

Diana Gleadhill worked as a professional librarian before becoming a graphic artist. Her leisure time is spent reading, gardening, sailing on Strangford Lough, and year-round walking in the Mourne Mountains with her life-long friend, Elise Coburn. Her natural curiosity and sense of adventure has taken her to such diverse destinations as Central Asia, Kenya, Papua New Guinea, South America and the Kamchatka Peninsula. She lives in County Down, Ireland.

Best Wishes
Diana Gleadhill

Our fiery hearts:
lust for knowing what may not be known

For Neil, Corin and Petra.
With all my love.

Diana Gleadhill

Our fiery hearts: Lust for knowing what may not be known

AUSTIN & MACAULEY

A CIP catalogue record for this title is available from the British Library.

ISBN 978 1 84963 086 3

www.austinmacauley.com

First Published (2011)
Austin & Macauley Publishers Ltd.
25 Canada Square
Canary Wharf
London
E14 5LB

Printed & Bound in Great Britain

Acknowledgements

Elise Coburn: My lifelong friend. I don't think either of us would ever go to the places we visit without each other. Thank you for your incomparable companionship, sometimes good sense and always humour! Thank you also for your excellent photos.

My thanks to all the following people without whose help I couldn't have written this book.

Billy Chittick: Yet again for your help with photographs.

Glenn and Steven Kennedy: For giving me so much time answering SOSs for help with maps, computer technical know-how and, indeed, my grammar!

Paul Craven and Steppes Travel: For all the patient advice and planning of most of our trips to Central Asia.

Somon Travel: For arranging our trip to Tajikistan despite our advanced years!

Odawni Palmer: For allowing me to use two verses of your poem about the Taklamakan Desert. The whole poem is simply lovely.

Chris Stillman. For yet again encouraging me to complete this book on Central Asia.

Cath Lindsay: My personal proof-reader who most tactfully made several amendments to the final manuscript.

Last, but by no means least. Mahasal Khan, Parvis Rakhimov and all the many other people of Central Asia who entertained us in their homes. To all of them, I extend my warmest thanks for their kindness and incredibly generous sense of hospitality.

Also by the Author:

We travel not for trafficking alone,
By hotter winds our fiery hearts are fanned.
For lust of knowing what may not be known,
We take the Golden Road to Samarkhand.

James Elroy Flecker.

CONTENTS

CENTRAL ASIA. POLITICAL

INTRODUCTION

When asked, to what do I attribute my infatuation with Central
Asia, I have to think right back, and suppose my fascination
started as a child. I had loved reading *The Far Distant Oxus* and,
The Oxus in Summer. Both these books were written by two
schoolgirls: Katherine Hull and Pamela Whitlock. When
enquiring of my parents where was 'The Oxus', they had to do a
bit of research. I had to be content when they told me the river
was now called the Amu Darya and was beyond Persia,
somewhere in far distant Asia.

Then, for my O Levels, I studied the epic Turks versus
Persians tragic poem by Matthew Arnold – *Sohrab and Rustum*. I
wept girlish tears over Sohrab's death at the hands of his father
not knowing that he had slain his son.

'... And he saw that Youth,
Of Age and Looks to be his own dear son,
Piteous and lovely, lying on the sand,
Like some rich hyacinth which by the scythe
Of an unskilful gardener has been cut,
Mowing the garden grass-plots near its bed,
And lies, a fragrant flower of purple bloom
On the mown dying grass so Sohrab lay,
Lovely in death, upon the common sand...'

A further fascination was the discovery – in an Encyclopaedia
of the Horse – of the Akhal-Teke. This is a slim-built, desert horse
from Turkmenistan. The sound of its name, the fact that it was
capable of journeying vast distances, and was probably one of the
fore-runners of our English Thoroughbred through the Byerly

Turk, the famous horse that came to England from Turkey in 1690, all remained in my memory.

A few years later, when I was nineteen and living and working in Washington DC, I enjoyed a short romance with a Persian student from Mashad in north-east Persia. His name was Abbass Motashari and was the son of a wealthy soldier in the Shah's army (that's also going back a bit). I was bowled-over by his dark good looks and the tales of his childhood with ethnic ties to, the then Soviet, Tajikistan. The very fact that it all seemed so impossibly distant and inaccessible, only whetted my appetite and curiosity about Central Asia.

Finally, many years later, I was off travelling as usual, with my childhood friend Elise Coburn. We had been on the Trans Mongolian Railway to China when we came upon a beautiful mosaic map of the Silk Road. It depicted the routes from China, around the Taklamakan Desert and through the High Pamirs to Central Asia and on towards the west. This really grabbed both our imaginations and we decided we would have to go and take a look for ourselves at some of these countries, which sounded so magically mysterious.

This knot of ancient lands in the heart of the largest landmass on Earth is unknown even today to many westerners. Its recorded history began in the 6th century BC when the huge Persian Empire created various 'kingdoms'. Khorezm, Margiana, Bactria, Saka, Arachosia, Aria and Sogdiana later known as Trans Oxiana by the Romans, meaning 'beyond the Oxus'. Gradually, through the years, Central Asia came under the control of other empires and place names and cultures changed.

The trans-continental routes of the Silk Road were known to have been in existence some five thousand years ago. The road started with the transportation of the beautiful blue stone – Lapis Lazuli – and the even more precious rock salt from Afghanistan. It wasn't until the 5th or 4th century BC that silk began to make an appearance beyond China. Using not one but a whole web of different routes around China's Taklamakan Desert and over Central Asia, the Silk Road wound westwards through Persia and on to the Mediterranean. In Central Asia great townships such as Bukhara, Samarkand, Merv, Osh and Kashgar became centres of commerce, art and science. Towards China, at the height of the Silk Road, camel trains carried horses, gold, ivory, precious metals, glass, fruit and vegetables. From China, came furs, ceramics, jade, lacquer work and of course the all important silk. But not only commodities were exchanged; international culture spread ideas, music, literature, art and religions. Trade was abandoned only in the mid 15th Century. Central Asia had split into Turkic and Mongol Khanates, and China had closed her doors against the rest of Asia, abandoning trade by both sea and land. By the 19th century a few camel trains carried tea from China and occasionally the Steppe nomads sold their horses to a few wandering Chinese.

During the late 1800s Tsarist Russia pushed her frontiers further south towards what is now Pakistan – at that time British India. The British, fearful that the Russians were intending to try and take India, retaliated against the Russians. The Great Game – the clandestine war between Russia and British India – was in full swing. The Russians, however, eventually succeeded in taking Bishkek in 1862, Tashkent 1865, Samarkand 1868, Kokand 1877 and Merv 1884. The fate of Central Asia was, for the time being, sealed.

It wasn't until the 1920s however – after the Russian Revolution – that the boundary lines on a map were drawn. These delineated the frontiers of the present day countries of Central Asia as we know them – Uzbekistan, Turkmenistan, Kazakhstan, Tajikistan and Kyrgistan. Afghanistan, Pakistan and the Xinjiang Province of Western China were also part of the Silk Road, but never came under Soviet domination. However, Stalin saw to it that Soviet Central Asia would not be tempted to unite and create an uprising. He skilfully gerrymandered the frontiers, so that 'dog-legs' of Uzbekistan, Tajikistan and Kyrgistan encroach into each other's territory – divide and rule was Stalin's credo. Today you will find plenty of Uzbeks in Turkmenistan and Tajikistan; Tajiks in Uzbekistan and Kyrgis in Tajikistan.

At the time, the Bolsheviks were hated. Their demands for food, livestock and cotton drained the countries of their once thriving trade and agriculture. Before and during the Second World War, collectivisation was introduced eliminating private property. Much of the vast Steppe was planted with wheat, robbing the nomadic peoples of Kazakstan and Kyrgistan of their lifestyles. The effect of this was disastrous. Millions died of starvation and disease. One way or another, Stalin's aim seemed to have been to depopulate the countries of Central Asia.

Nevertheless, for all the early atrocities that happened in Central Asia during Soviet times, later, there were many benefits. Health care, education and the whole infrastructure were improved. Everybody had employment and old folk were rewarded for their labours with reasonable pensions. Women had economic and educational equality and art and literature were taught, encouraging national identities.

In Afghanistan, the ten-year guerrilla war waged between the Afghans and Soviet Russia, eventually ended in 1989 with the Russian's ignominious retreat. The cost in lives and money to each side was enormous, very probably exacerbating the break-up of the Soviet Union. In 1991, along with other Soviet satellite countries, the countries of Central Asia declared their independence.

So now, we wondered, after many centuries of subjugation under different rulers, how were people coping with independence? What were the countries like? How did the people live? Curiosity, as ever, drove us to see for ourselves.

As a pair of spritely sixty-year-olds, Elise and I first set foot in Central Asia in 1998. We set out as a couple of 'tourists', but it wasn't long before the 'tourists' metamorphosed into involved and curious 'travellers'.

My late friend and neighbour, Malcolm Gordon, was always interested in geography and hence Elise's and my peregrinations over the globe. He had shown me pictures in the National Geographic magazine of the opening of the Karakoram Highway in 1986 and together with Elise, we thought what a great way to start our travels to Central Asia. Our initial intention was to start in Pakistan, up the KKH into China, then turn left into Tajikistan and on to Uzbekistan for Samarkand and Bukhara. However, by the time we were ready to leave, Tajikistan was in the midst of a bitter civil war, so we had to re-think our route. We went instead, as already planned, up the KKH and over the Kunjerab Pass into the Xynjiang Region of western China. But then, instead of going west, we continued north into the Tien Shan, or Mountains of Heaven, over the Torugart Pass into Kyrgistan. Then, finally, west into Uzbekistan, to the old cities of Bukhara and Samarkand, thus circumnavigating Tajikistan – at least for the present.

However, as we travelled we became more and more interested in the people. In Northern Pakistan we met wonderful folk. But our progress up the Karakorum Highway was almost totally dominated by the terrain and the construction of this extraordinary road. Kyrgistan proved to be rather an anachronism in that we didn't actually experience much of the Kyrgis people – all we met were Russians. In Uzbekistan we reverted to being 'bona fide tourists' visiting Samarkand and Bukhara and mostly meeting Tajiks. The one Uzbek guide we had, proved to be a complete non-starter. Perhaps an expression of his cultural antipathy towards independent women!

Nevertheless, we did learn a lot about the people of these countries and how we related to them. So we determined, there and then to return to Central Asia as soon as Tajikistan's civil war was ended. However, various reasons conspired to postpone our return until ten and a half years later. In 2009, two almost-as-spritely seventy-one-year-olds finally set off for Turkmenistan and Tajikistan, where, in both countries – we stayed several times with the local people – a huge learning curve, both about them – and about ourselves.

We would, inadvertently, have left the best, or worst, till last!

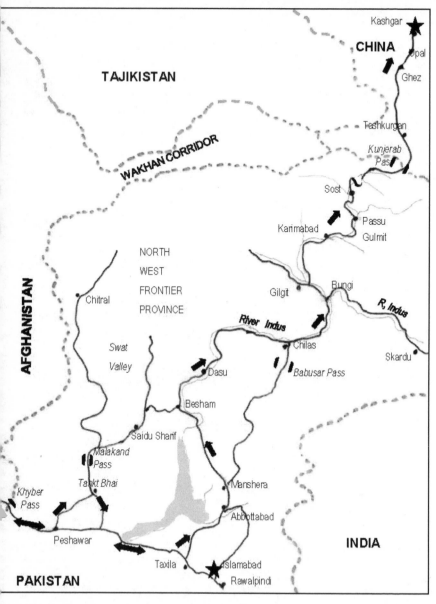

NORTHERN PAKISTAN and the KARAKORUM HIGHWAY   Our Route

NORTHERN PAKISTAN
1998

When spring-time flushes the desert grass,
Our kafilas wind through the Khyber Pass.
Lean are the camels, but fat the frails,
Light are the purses but heavy the bales.
As the snow-bound trade of the north comes down
To the market-square in Peshawur town.

Rudyard Kipling, 1865 – 1936

Peshawar. A Scary Start.

The tall, fair-haired young man turned around from the reception desk.

"Hi," he greeted us, "are you checking-out too?"

"No, no", we responded, "we've only just arrived".

"Well, you shouldn't be here. There's a warning out that all Europeans and especially Americans must leave the country."

"What on earth are you talking about?" we asked.

"There's been a strike by the Americans in Kabul and the authorities are afraid there may be possible reprisals from Afghan sympathizers here in Pakistan. I think you should get the hell outa here."

Wow! For sure this Dutch reporter was very agitated insisting we should go home, but it didn't really sink in what he was saying. For a start, like a pair of idiots, we thought of a 'strike' as 'going off work'. However, it did transpire that the Americans had launched a missile strike into Kabul in retaliation for the bombing earlier in the summer, in Nairobi. But when we asked Yousef, our guide, about this disturbing news, he knew nothing –

or at least, said he knew nothing – about it at all. Ignorance, as they say, is bliss, and we put the whole incident right out of our minds.

Elise and I had arrived the day before, at Islamabad Airport near the old town of Rawalpindi – or, as the old school would say 'Pindi'. We were met at the airport by Yousef, while we were in Pakistan, and driven the hundred miles or so along the Great Trunk Road to Peshawar. In ancient times there was a settlement called Purushapura somewhere in the area of Peshawar established by the Kushans. Today's city of Peshawar – which in Persian means 'High Fort' – was established in the 16th century during the Mughal period by Akbar. It had always been a main trading place on the ancient Silk Road. Today, it is the capital of the North West Frontier Province and the economic, cultural and political capital of the Pashtuns in Pakistan. Close to Afghanistan it is an often violent border town full, I am sure, of some pretty shady characters. The trading nowadays, is still in carpets but also in opium and arms.

En route we went through the area of Gandara in the Hero River Valley, to visit the museum and excavation site of the ancient city of Taxila, where Alexander the Great came in 327 BC when it was still a province of the Achaemenian Empire. However, we were both so exhausted by the journey that we really didn't take it all in and were glad to continue our drive to Peshawar. After the initial shock at the sign in the lobby inviting everyone with firearms to please leave them at reception, we found our hotel, the Pearl Continental and our room cool and comfortable and had a very necessary bath and snooze.

However, it wasn't long before we ventured out to explore a little of Peshawar. It was very, very hot – 39 degrees and 80% humidity and I was conscious of the pearls of sweat beading my forehead. We wanted to buy some fruit juice and the *shalwar kameez*, the cool, airy loose shirt and baggy trousers favoured by the local people. We had a hilarious time trying to find men's clothing; more practical for the journey we were about to do. The shop keepers simply couldn't understand why we would want to wear plain men's clothes when we could be getting dolled up in some of the gorgeous fancy ladies wear. However, finally we found what we wanted and made our purchases. There was by this time, an army of small boys bouncing along with us practicing their English which usually amounted to 'Hallo, how are you?' and then giggling like mad. Some of them were quite bold and knew enough English to have a short conversation. It was, as ever, great fun.

That evening we ate in sublime comfort – a mixed dinner – partly European and partly Pakistani, but delicious. Very tired, we repaired to bed early with the exciting thought that in the morning, we would visit the Khyber Pass!

The Khyber Pass. Doesn't the very name conjure up rugged mountains, soldiers, Afghan rebels – somewhere one has always known of but never, never thought to visit, and here we were about to go there. The pass itself is a 53 km/33 mi long passage through the Hindu Kush – 'Killer of Hindus' – connecting Pakistan and Afghanistan. At its narrowest point it is only 3 m/9.8 ft wide. The pass has a long and often violent history but for hundreds of years has been a major trade route.

We had first to collect an armed guard at his barracks. He appeared. A slight black-bearded man, dressed totally in black – from beret to sandals – and very well armed with a huge AK45. Then off we went, westwards through part of the North West Frontier Province. There were many, many Afghan refugees living, or camping, in the area. All along the roadside were shops and stalls filled with goods brought in, duty free, from Afghanistan. All manner of merchandise, from textiles to tyres, and beds to bicycles. Hundreds of bikes being ridden with a string of more bikes on tow. And *firearms*, sold absolutely openly from road-side stalls – hundreds of them. Amazing. We could photograph anything we wanted except the women, but as there hardly were any anyway, and those we saw were heavily veiled under their *burkas*, there wasn't too much temptation.

As we got to the outskirts of Peshawar for the two hour journey, we had to stop at a police check-point. Yousef took our passports and papers into the building. Suddenly, a man came pelting along towards us, at his heels, a bevy of men shaking sticks and shouting. Our driver and the guard jumped out of the car and joined in the charge, disappearing without a backward glance, leaving Elise and me alone and quite bewildered. Should we get out and run also? Should we try and find Yousef? It was just a mite scary, wondering what on earth was afoot. It wasn't long, however, before all three of our men returned to report that a man had been seen stealing a gun and so everyone had given chase. Well. What with our warnings to leave the country and now this escapade, such a lot of excitement so soon? Whatever next?

As we drove along we passed many lorries carrying purple onions, tobacco, tea and of all things, rocks. As we climbed ever higher, we stopped from time to time to look at the views and take photographs. At one such place we fell in with a Chinese American who verified the Dutch reporter's story and told us to 'get the hell out of the country as soon as you can'. He reckoned he was probably OK as he looked more Chinese than American unless they looked at his passport, but he was most concerned for our safety. Again, neither Yousef nor even the armed guard seemed to think there was any sort of a problem.

Amazingly there is a train line – no doubt a relic from the days of the Brits – from Peshawar to the pass, zigzagging up the mountains. We had originally thought about taking the train, but apparently it has now been closed to passenger travel. So excepting the odd steam train engine excursion, this mode of transport was definitely out. Before we got to the pass we came to the spot where the regimental crests of the battalions who fought here adorn the rock face. We took photos and felt very moved at where we were and the skirmishes that had gone on here in this strange land so far from home and so long ago.

The pass itself is very dramatic. Having wound our way up the mountains and passed ancient forts and gone through villages, we came to a high spot on the road, and quite suddenly the road falls away off downhill, corkscrewing down into Afghanistan. It was hot and still and rather hazy and so apparently innocuous. We posed for photos looking very intimidating wearing the guard's heavy rifle and chatted to some boys who had arrived out of nowhere. Again, these boys spoke pretty good English, which is such an advantage to us as we can converse with people. We got talking to our guard who had a great face, long and narrow with a long aquiline nose and astonishingly, the most amazingly blue eyes. He asked me my name and age (a bit forward I thought) and when I told him, he said I had a very good body! (Even more forward I thought.) I was a bit gob-smacked, I thought these people were rather reserved especially with women, of course I have to say I was quite chuffed – hah! Am I not easily pleased?

Ever since we arrived in Northern Pakistan, Elise and I had been fascinated by the vehicles. They were of all kinds, massively decorated with bright designs, so to Yousef's absolute astonishment we asked him if we could see how it was done. Consequently, in the afternoon we set off through Peshawar to the district where you would find tradesmen – blacksmiths, mechanics, plumbers and so on, where we found the Vehicle Enhancing Yard. The lorries would start off with just a chassis and cab and a gang would build the whole vehicle. It's a very busy industry and customers have their lorries personalised with their own combination of designs. The wooden frames are covered with plastic sections of brilliant colours – birds, flowers, curlicues, Islamic art, frills etc. A lot of pieces are mirror-plastic reflecting the lights at night. The doors and part of the cab are beautifully and intricately carved in wood. The garage we went to was very surprised that we wanted to see their work. All the workers were friendly and helpful and described how they put together their vehicles in which, needless to say they took a great pride. After the tour of the lorries we were seated and given mugs of very sweet tea. We of course were also great objects of curiosity and had to tell them all about our families and our jobs and lifestyle.

Naturally enough, no visit to Pakistan is complete without a visit to a carpet factory. I expect the guides are all in line for a bit of a back-hander from the factory if they make a sale. Elise was actually intending to buy a rug anyway and we had great fun looking at all the different carpets. She wanted one for her hall, which is long and narrow. After lots of tea-drinking and discussions about duty and postage, the serious haggling began in earnest. Eventually Elise was still hovering over the cost of a very pretty pink rug, saying she really didn't want to go over a certain price when I butted in and said to the pushy wee salesman, "This is her final price." And hoping like mad he would accept it, we got up as if to go. Luckily he did settle at her price and promised she would not have to pay duty. (Weeks later when we were back home, her carpet arrived OK but sadly she did have to pay duty.)

After all this excitement Yousef handed us over to a chum of his called Manzoor. He was going to take us to one of our favourite places – the old market while Yousef had a few hours respite from his two exhausting ladies! He took us slowly through the teeming alleyways. Like all bazaars it was filled with everything you could possibly think of. In the food market there was rice of all sorts, and exotic smelling tobacco also of many different types, in great big sacks. Lentils, saffron and nuts – and – poppy heads, now I wonder what they could be used for? In another area there was clothing. Boots, shoes, loads of sandals and hundreds of hats of all sorts of shapes and sizes. Hats seemed to be a prerequisite for nearly all the men we had noticed. It didn't appear that many tourists ever came here as absolutely nobody hassled us. People were curious about us but mostly smiled, and the children again asked "how are you?" They just seemed to be pleasant, friendly people. We were reminded several times a day that we were in an Islamic country as we heard the Muezzin's sonorous tones chanting out 'Allah Akbar' – God is Great – as he called the faithful to prayer.

While we had been on the plane, during our flight here, Elise found herself sitting next to a Pakistani gentleman and naturally they struck up a conversation. He was charming and told us his name was Mahasal, a widower who amazingly came from Peshawar. He ended up inviting us to his home for dinner some evening that suited us. We announced this to Yousef when we arrived back in the hotel. He was absolutely appalled and said we couldn't possibly go out with a man we had only just met. We felt like two schoolchildren and told him we would be perfectly OK. He was not to be budged and to our unending embarrassment he insisted on being with us when Mahasal came to collect us from the hotel. I suppose you could forgive him as he was, after all, responsible for us.

We dressed ourselves up as smartly as the clothes we had allowed and went to reception to meet our new friend. We wondered if, in fact, he would turn up. Would we recognise him as he had been wearing western clothes on the plane, and we thought he might be wearing the *shalwar kameez*. We need not have worried, he was already waiting for us, with a gorgeous little grandson in his arms. There, also, was Yousef, so of course we had to introduce him. Yousef insisted on following us to Mahasal's house, and said he would wait for us and bring us back, but Mahasal said he didn't know what time we would be ready and that he would bring us back to the hotel. It was really cringe-making. We thought he and Yousef were going to have a row on our behalf, but Yousef backed down and said he would be waiting in reception until we returned. We were so embarrassed, but Mahasal took it all very calmly and off we set.

The Khan home was a huge house set in the rather exclusive military, banking and diplomatic area. It had nine bedrooms all with bathrooms en suite. There were five servants to look after

Mahasal, his pretty daughter Maimouna and her little son. They were the most delightful people one could wish to meet. We had a wonderful dinner all cooked by Maimouna. Somewhat alarmingly there was no cutlery, so we watched how our hosts managed – fingers of course, and a basin and towel at the ready on a side board. Maimoona's husband was a doctor and doing further studies in, of all places, Dublin. Her's had been an arranged marriage, but she had consented to it and obviously loved and missed her husband. She was amazed when we said we were free to choose our husbands in the West – some for better, some, sadly, for worse. They were a very well-educated family, Mahasal a grower of sugar-cane and a banker, spoke perfect English having travelled extensively. Maimouna, surprisingly, used to work before she had her baby, could drive a car and was very emancipated. We had such an interesting evening of chat, touching of course, on religion, third world poverty and first world power.

The house was decorated in muted colours of cream and brown, really surprising as Maimouna wore a beautiful *shalwar* and jewelry, and when we saw the photos of her wedding, they had had it in a tent (not quite like ours) in the garden, lavishly decorated with splendid, Islamic-designed wall hangings and carpets. Perhaps it is more dignified to have western furniture and décor rather than the brilliant national décor.

In any case what a privilege it was to have met this family and been entertained at their home in Peshawar. When Mahasal returned us safe and sound to our hotel, there indeed was our faithful guardian. Yousef, true to his word, had waited diligently to see his two loose women safely returned to his care. We packed a fair lot into this day. Needless to say, this being a Muslim country there is no alcohol around, however we were able to rectify this lack from our own little duty-free cache.

Well... the following was a very interesting day! Ending up, not at all where we should have been. Our itinerary said *'a gentle day to Saidu Sharif'*. We started out early in the morning, going north. En route we stopped at the Takht-i-Bahi monastery, which at 1500 years old, was one of the largest Buddhist temples in India. It was still boiling hot and we had to climb hundreds of steps to reach the ruins. It was well worth it, for the view was marvellous. The monastery is situated in the middle of a plain but on top of a small hill, putting it in a brilliantly strategic position with panoramic views all round. Takht-i-Bahi was established as an UNESCO World Heritage Site in 1980.

On we went over the Malacan Pass and down into the Swat Valley. We had only just begun to enjoy this beautiful place when we were stopped by the police, and told that we had to turn back as it was too dangerous for Europeans to continue to Saidu Sharif.

It appeared that the Dutch reporter was quite right. The Afghans bombed by the Americans were now, naturally, angry and on the war path for any western people, in particular Americans. The Swat valley runs north parallel to the border with Afghanistan and many families and tribes spill over from one country into another, hence there are a lot of Afghan sympathizers in Pakistan. Although they were really looking for Americans, if they had seen a white face, they were hardly going to stop and ask to see your passport! We were a bit shaken by this news, and of course disappointed that we could not continue up the valley. However, we were unfazed and pretty philosophical about things, after all we came from Northern Ireland where we have had to put up with years of 'troubles'. The next vehicle to arrive after us was a lorry belonging to Explore Worldwide and full of young people and their leader/driver who was *totally* furious by having all her plans thwarted. A large, bossy girl, she got really stroppy in the police station and started to throw her considerable weight about, threatening all sorts of action and going on – dare I say it – in a rather Brit sort of way. I imagine, actually, she was pretty scared. The lorry was open-sided leaving the occupants very vulnerable.

Yousef said there was no other way but to retrace our steps. He persuaded the Explore girl also to return from whence we had come, getting out of the Swat valley as soon as possible, and joining the Karakorum Highway at its official beginning.

Up until now we had thought of Fridoun, our driver, as the calmest and most careful of drivers. But the thought of us being hijacked lent wings to his wheels and was just the excuse needed to show how exciting his skill at speed-driving could be! We tied scarves round our heads to hide the colour of our hair, drew the curtains in the minibus and set off at a rate of knots back the way we had come. Without a doubt this was to be one of the scariest drives either of us had ever had. There were indeed several road blocks of angry, gesticulating people. We were forced to take little unpaved side roads to avoid being stopped along with four other vehicles fleeing like us. We left the Explore people far behind. At one block we had to reverse away over a rickety little bridge and along the grassy bank of a river, both of us lying on the floor praying we wouldn't be stopped. Yousef's body language said it all. He sat on the edge of his seat peering ahead and giving instructions in a staccato voice to Fridoun. We attacked the Malakan Pass with its tortuous bends, overtaking other transport and taking absolutely wild risks. Elise and I grimaced at each other from time to time, hanging on for grim death as we rolled around the floor. I finally said I'd rather take my chances with the Afghans than risk certain death going over the edge of the mountain. My protests fell on stony ground and we belted on until about four o'clock, when at last we stopped for a late lunch at a little café. All we actually wanted was drink – of the soft sort. We set off again going a little gentler, still covered up but a bit more relaxed. Whew!

We didn't have to go all the way back to Peshawar but turned off to join the Highway at its start – Taxila. By the time we got there it was dark and we discussed the pros and cons of continuing. In the event we went as far as Abbottabad, so named in deference to Captain James Abbott, a major player in the Great

Game. We stopped there for a very good Chinese meal around 10 o'clock, intending to continue to Besham for the night. However, Besham is quite near Saidu Sharif where we were earlier and it was possible the same tribesmen would be causing more road blocks. Consequently we decided to stay at Mansehra for the night, giving us more options for our northern progress the next day. We were told the road ahead was OK, but we would know better in the morning. If there were any problems we should have to hire a Land Rover and try and negotiate the Babusar Pass, quite a difficult hike, much of it probably on foot.

Even with all the excitement of the day I was terribly sleepy and had nodded off from time to time in my customary fashion, to Elise's great frustration. Our room here was grand and we were both glad to fall into bed.

Karakorum Highway to Gilgit and a Polo Match
We awoke to wonderful birdsong in the trees outside our room. By now quite high up, it was much cooler and raining. While we were having breakfast I spied a rat sitting on the curtain pole opposite me. I waited until Yousef joined us and then I drew his attention to it. "My God, oh my God," his reaction was so funny. He was absolutely horrified and yelled at the staff to do something about it. They leisurely took a look at it and at us and sniggered together, then they got a big stick and started poking at it. The rat, of course, jumped down and proceeded to scuttle around eliciting shrieks from the other breakfasters including Yousef. What fun, it lent a whole new meaning to the expression 'rat race'!

Our morning drive took us through rich agricultural land. Rice, wheat and vegetables. Pine trees, birches and blackberries. Through small villages and roadside bazaars all busy with a great cross-section of people, mostly men wearing the same great variety of headgear that we had seen in the market in Peshawar. Old men with white turbans and red-dyed beards. There were skull-caps, short round fez's and the very popular sort of round, flat, pancake job with rolled over edges. The River Indus flowed towards us down a deep ravine, grey and silt-laden from the high glaciers, eventually to deposit its riches on the lowlands of southern Pakistan. Every so often we came across cable cars across the ravine to transport people from one side of the valley to the other. We took a ride in one such battered cable car swinging perilously across the wildly swirling river. On we went into the area of Indus Kohistan. The hills were now becoming much steeper and the mud slides started. Downhill into Besham for lunch. The sun was shining again and it was hot.

All afternoon we followed the Indus on the Karakorum Highway for a totally mind-blowing drive. We went through this gorge, 40 km/24.8 mi long, on a road, literally hacked out of the sheer cliff face. Often we were as much as 1,000 m/3,000 ft above the river. It is absolutely astonishing. This section of the road, apparently, claimed hundreds of labourers' lives. Sometimes it seemed there wouldn't be room for us under the overhang, and we would duck our heads involuntarily, of course there was room for us, after all, local buses and lorries use this same spectacular route all the time.

Begun in 1958, just after Pakistan's independence, the KKH as it is known, was built to connect Pakistan with China, its ally against India. It has to be one of the most extraordinary feats of engineering ever attempted. So dangerous was the daunting job of hewing this road from the unforgiving terrain, that it cost the life of one navvy for each of its four hundred kilometres. As progress on the road almost came to a standstill, in 1968 the Chinese came to the rescue. They were anxious to make an easy route to the markets of Pakistan for their massive output of merchandise. Christened, 'The Friendship Highway', the road was finally completed in 1978.

We descended again to river level, and the geography changed. Here the river flows through a broad valley with huge sand dunes on the far side. Always we were conscious of the massive bulk of mountains all around us. Nanga Parbat, at 9000 m/29,527 ft lay to the east on our right hand side, being part of the Himalayas, whilst to the left were the Hindu Kush.

We spent the night at the Shangri La Hotel, rather ill-described as it was a bit of a hick joint, but everyone seemed pleasant and friendly. We were still unable to leave the hotel or go for a walk as everyone was nervous about there being trouble over the colour of our skin. So, nothing for it but to have a small consolation in the privacy of our room.

The following day, once again the scenery changed. We stopped to have a look at the Buddhist petroglyphs and hot springs bubbling down the hillside and on to the road. This hot water moving all the time adds to the instability of the area. There were indeed a lot of mud slides, and huge falls on either side of the road, of stones just held together with mud, and all looking very fragile. It was extraordinary. This road cutting through these massive mountains, which are always on the move. Frequent earthquakes occur with the accompanying landslips and avalanches. We arrived at a spot where we had a really good view of Nanga Parbat, part of it's towering peak just slightly hidden by cloud, but the remainder shining with snow. At 8,126 m/26,660 ft, Nanga Parbat is one of the greatest challenges to mountaineers, and has been the cause of so many deaths that it is known as Killer Mountain.

There is a lookout spot on the side of the road just here, where the three great mountain ranges come together. It is dramatically obvious. On the right, the Himalayas gently sweep down from the east to meet the Hindu Kush to the west. They are both dwarfed at this point by the back-drop of the black, spiky, intimidating bulk of the Karakorums.

We arrived in Gilgit and booked into a little hotel, which was really nice with a lovely garden smelling of apricots and a wonderful view of Rakaposhi. Here we were at 2,500 m/5,000 ft and had now left the Indus, which turns off eastwards towards Baltistan. We were now travelling alongside the Gilgit River. After lunch we went for a really steep climb up the hillside over a rough path, which was reasonably easy going. There were interesting, rather intimate views over the backs of little houses and gardens. We soon hit farming land and small-holdings, grazing some cattle and growing potatoes and maize.

We had expressed the desire to Yousef, if it would be possible, to see a polo match as we thought this was the very place where polo came from. To our great delight he came up trumps and told us there would be a match in the late afternoon.

This turned out to be a real bonus. The polo ground was a long narrow 'field' of sand and dust in a natural amphitheatre, the mountains around touched with the golden light of late afternoon. It appeared that the ponies quite often used to jump the low concrete wall surrounding the field, and people were getting hurt so a wire-netting fence was added for protection. There were no other women in the crowd and we sat conspicuously between an old man and some little boys who spent most of the time sizing us up, nudging each other and giggling. On the opposite side of the arena a band played all afternoon. It consisted of pipes and drums and when we arrived there was a man in the arena doing an extraordinary dance. Lots of whirling around, slow elegant hand movements and shoulder shaking. It appeared to be quite spontaneous.

There was such an atmosphere of excited expectation and when the players appeared there was a great deal of cheering and shouting – us included. One side played straight into the low, hazy sun. The whole place was such a dust bowl that how any of the audience, let alone the players, saw the ball, was a mystery. The ponies looked to be in great condition but were not changed, as at home, at the end of a chukka. They wore far less equipment than western polo-ponies and the players wore neither helmets nor knee guards. There appeared to be no rules – it just seemed to be a gigantic free-for-all and all the more fun for that. At half time and at the end of the match we were entertained to more of the spontaneous dancing, followed by a prize-giving ceremony. Prizes were awarded to the winning home team by a local dignitary. We hung around for quite some time taking photos and getting a closer look at the ponies. They are tough and strong with, I should say a lot of Arab blood and lovely, little curly tipped ears. The steam rising from their sweaty bodies had the familiar smell of our horses at home.

The bazaar in Gilgit was a delight. So many little shops with so much interesting merchandise and shopkeepers who didn't hassle but who were keen to show you all they had to offer. We were lucky enough to be invited into the back of one stall – which was like a little house – with shy women-folk, curious kids and numerous cups of tea. We were glad to have a whole afternoon free of Yousef. He was beginning to irritate us with his schoolmasterish attitude. He didn't seem to realize that we like to be independent and not to be treated as though on a school outing. However he took us to see fresh *nan bread* being made. Rolled-out dough stuck on to the inside wall of the oven for a few minutes, and Bob's your uncle, it's ready to eat – delicious.

The Naltar Valley, about 40 km/24.8 mi from Gilgit, is renowned for its wildlife and stunning scenery. Due to a quirk of climate it receives much more rain than Gilgit, enabling good pine and some deciduous forestation. Because this is up a *really* rough road – even rougher than we had been used to, and very steep – we had to take a jeep and a local driver. This journey was definitely not for the faint-hearted, along a very narrow, very bumpy track clinging to the mountain-side. Sometimes at river level, sometimes 100 metres above it. Often mud and stones obliterating the track. Some of the walls of the road looked so fragile, just soft grey clay holding together round pebbles, and this on the *river* side of the track! Shit scary. A beautiful, clear tumbling river whooshed down, the icy coldness of it creating a deliciously cool up-current of air. Lots of trembling wee bridges to cross until three hours later we were at 9000 feet in a small Alpine valley. It was very, very pretty; green fields of corn, rice and potatoes. Everywhere irrigation ditches brought water bubbling along from much higher up, down to quench the valley below. Walnut, poplar and apricot trees lent patches of welcome shade here and there. Some of the houses, we noticed, were built right into the sides of the hill, with no windows. Cooler in the hot summer, and possibly not too paralysingly cold in the bitter winters.

We went off to have a good walk and to explore the houses and the crops. Before having a picnic lunch Yousef was doing one of his bossy acts; telling us not to sit where we had chosen beside a little stream. He treated us like a pair of real idiots, maybe he is used to recalcitrant tour groups. Anyway we chose to ignore him and stayed where we were. I swore that if he went on like that we would end up having a row.

After lunch we stopped at a little tea-house for green tea, and, as it was looking like rain to put the roof up on the jeep. Our driver was lovely, very handsome and wearing a dashing red bandana round his head. He was quite chatty and informative when we asked him questions and when he could get a word in before Yousef. Elise and I decided at this point that we would forego the tea and walk on down the hill while the men struggled with the roof and had their tea. They would pick us up farther down the track. We had a lovely walk for a couple of hours. The only person we passed was a man leading a donkey loaded up with firewood. In fact it was so well loaded that you couldn't see the donkey, just a bundle of sticks with four legs. It was so quiet there, not another vehicle appeared, just the rushing river and the great peaks for company.

Back again in the jeep we approached Gilgit and went to cross the bridge, but were stopped by a youth who said the bridge was 'one way' from the other side. Well... Yousef really lost the plot. He was furious, shouting and gesticulating and went to get out of the jeep and would have had a punch at the lad if it hadn't been for the driver restraining him. He had remained calm and quiet throughout the fracas. Of course we couldn't understand what it was all about at the time, but really Yousef did not acquit himself at all well. He could not bear to lose face, but it was such bad behaviour and so unnecessary, and we told him so.

Entranced by the bazaar we had a lovely time again, chatting and making little purchases and drinking tea with the stallholders. Back at the hotel we did a good old wash, hanging our smalls indecently on the balcony and having a relaxing sundowner gazing in awe at Rakaposhi, brilliant in the evening, perfectly clear and pink-tinged from the setting sun.

Of course, in the evening, as if to atone for all past misdemeanours, Yousef excelled himself by taking us to a local restaurant. He was a different person, in great form and ordering a variety of dishes for us to sample. We ate outdoors. You couldn't say in a courtyard, more a back yard of a garage-cum-restaurant, where people came and went, and drove pick-ups in and out. All very busy. The food was delicious. No knife and fork, so everything was eaten in ones' fingers, picked up in a sort of untidy way between two pieces of *nan bread*. Fridoun was with us, which was nice as he was part of our little team. He was gentle and smiley and always on time. We were also joined by a local sort of doctor. Yousef said he was a quack but we talked to him quite a bit and I think he practiced some sort of alternative medicine – Pakistan style.

A telephone call for Elise, first thing the following morning, woke us up. It was from the colonel who was organizing our time in Pakistan. He asked very solicitously after us and congratulated us on being such 'stalwart' ladies after our bad experience in the Swat Valley! He said how admirably we had behaved and how impressed Yousef had been when we didn't panic. Gosh, praise indeed. We said that of course we came from Ireland and were quite used to road blocks and civil disturbance. Frankly we were very, very scared – Northern Ireland is one thing, Pakistan quite another.

To our horror, some time after we arrived back home, Elise was sent the cutting of a feature in The Telegraph written by an undercover reporter stating that a reward of $15,000 had been offered by the Afghans, for any American captured – alive or dead. The reporter, Carlos Mavroleon, heir to a vast fortune, who had been educated at Eton and Harvard, was discovered – dead – exactly one week after we had been in Peshawar. He had been found in his room at the cheap Green's Hotel having been seen exiting the Pearl Continental earlier that day. The report said he died from an alleged overdose, but the general consensus of opinion was that he was in fact murdered. Were we lucky or what? We had taken very little notice of the warnings given us by two sources. It was also very remiss of Yousef not to have taken the warnings seriously and, at the very least clarified the situation.

KKH and a Huge Landslide.
Off then again up the KKH. The road wound through a wide plain with alluvial fans spilling down the mountainside. Again pockets of grass among the dun coloured rocks and scree. Rock slides again, everything soaking wet from ice melting *inside* the rocks… ho humm.

One time when we arrived at a police checkpoint we witnessed a horrible bicycle accident. A tourist flying downhill hit a mini van, which had pulled out to pass us. Ending up in a heap, with bike and luggage in a tangle, the young man lay clutching his shoulder. We left, as we were not actually involved. I felt a bit mean not staying to help sort things out, I just hoped the guy had some insurance as it looked as though he might have broken his collar bone. Although this area has schools and healthcare funded by the Aga Khan Foundation, both apparently excellent, I don't think I'd really like to be in an accident.

A great deal of work is done through the Aga Khan Foundation. The foundation is a private, international, non-denominational, non-governmental organization, operating in many countries especially Africa and Asia regardless of colour or creed. Founded in 1967, the foundation concentrates its resources on selected issues, particularly in health, education, rural development and the strengthening of civil society. It tries to identify solutions that can be adapted to local conditions in the many different regions. The present Aga Khan is the 49th hereditary spiritual leader of the Shia Ismaili Muslims. We found that the people in northern Pakistan revere him, his portrait being portrayed in many homes and businesses.

We continued on to a little restaurant on the side of the road for morning tea. It was in the most beautiful situation near a sparkling stream bordered with pretty, delicate flowering cosmos in all shades of pinks and mauves. The stream was the melt water flowing down from the Rakaposhi glacier. Unfortunately it was a little cloudy just hiding a clear view of the summit We met some Australian tourists and compared notes with them. It's interesting talking about travel with other people, what they get out of it and why they do it. When I said how difficult it was to describe things to people back home, a man replied, "Travel is for yourself. You just tell those folks to git up off of their asses and go see it for their selves."

Of course it's absolutely true. It is such a learning curve with each new place you go and the different people you meet – the climate, politics, way of life. It is a humbling and enlarging experience at the same time. We discovered the group had been over the Babusar Pass. We had very nearly done it from necessity after the Swat valley fracas, but they had done it for the *hell* of it. Apparently it was really difficult, terribly cold and with very rough going, to the extent that one woman said she had had enough and wanted to go home, to the dismay of her husband. But she insisted and so their departure had to be organized. What a shame, I'm sure if she had persisted and continued on, she would have enjoyed the rest of this journey.

There were some stalls here tempting the odd passing tourist. We bought some rather nice crystals.

Our next stop was not on schedule. Four or five miles further up the road we came across a huge landslide. There was a long queue of vehicles waiting so we got out of the car and walked up to where the action was. A few men with pick axes, crowbars and shovels were doing their best to remove mud and boulders. Every so often they would succeed in prizing a huge boulder off the path and send it tumbling over the edge of the road, down to the river far below. I stood for quite a while watching fascinated, under a perilous looking overhang just waiting to fall. Meantime, Elise pushed her way through the other spectators to take photographs. It was pointless waiting in the queue as it was obviously going to take some time to clear the fall – the largest so far that we had seen. So we returned to the restaurant we had previously been at, to have lunch and to wait. We paddled in the river, which was freezing but deliciously refreshing, and went for a good climb up the river-bank towards the glacier with Rakaposhi now totally clear, making a side-trip to the local 'long-drop'. Talk about a loo with a view.

By the time we returned to the road the landslide was cleared by the KKH maintenance team so we were able to continue onwards. Suddenly Fridoun came to a grinding halt, jumped out of the car and started kicking around in the gravel at the side of the road. There were also two little boys doing the same thing. They came rushing over to us with handfuls of what looked like grubby little stones. They were rough garnets scooped up from the roadside. The lads hoped we might buy them, but we had a much better idea and joined Fridoun, scratching about for the small, dusty gems.

We were now at a height of about 3000 metres so felt quite leaden legged and a little headachy when we arrived at Karimabad. However, nothing daunted, after a long glass of water, we decided to go off for a walk. Everywhere was the sound of rushing water from streams and irrigation ditches, plus the noise of the main Hunza River far below. There was the sweet smell of apricots all the time, for although the season was nearly over, and there were large baskets on the flat roofs with apricots drying in the sun, there were quite a lot still unpicked on the trees looking so pretty. Plum, apple and walnut trees were also cultivated, with the river banks lined by Poplars.

From our hotel balcony at drinks time, we looked down over a patchwork of green and gold fields. We could make out, far below us, a family gathering potatoes, working their way gradually down the field. We could see where a trailer had overturned from the back of a tractor and spilled a whole lot of sacks of grain, the golden load smeared over the road. Women and children were busy sweeping it up, but the wind kept blowing it away. Everything looked so healthy; the short-stalked wheat stood amazingly upright, unlike the battered grain at home. We had dinner on the terrace accompanied by a band playing local music – the heat of the day evaporating into the clear, starry sky, leaving it chilly at night.

Two Old Forts and the Hoper Glaciar

The following day was dull and cloudy, so Yousef and the local guide had decided we couldn't go up to the Hopar glacier and decided to visit the Altit and Baltit forts instead. After breakfast I discovered the sole was coming off one of my decrepit but comfy shoes, so left the pair at reception to go to the cobblers. When I got them back at lunchtime they were gleaming clean and *both* had been beautifully mended, at a cost of only 30 rupees.

Altit fort was nearly a ruin. It was built about 1100 as a Mir's palace. It has a wonderfully strategic position looking up and down the valley high above the river. Immediately below are the houses of the descendants of the Mir's servants, their flat roofs covered with drying apricots. It was lovely, almost nobody else was there and the whole place was full of ancient mystery with its carved doorways and crumbling stone-pillared passageways. We approached the fort through a beautiful, irrigated garden, full of vines and apricot, apple and plum trees.

Baltit fort is at the top of dozens of steep steps, quite exhausting to climb at this altitude but well worth the effort. We had to join a large German group for a guided tour, and were reprimanded for going off at a tangent on our own! (We're not very good with tour groups.) The fort has been very well restored by the Aga Khan Trust after a survey by the Royal Geographical Society of London. It is now a museum and furnished with artifacts from the early 1900s. The foundations of the fort are said to date back around 700 years, but there have been rebuilds and alterations over the centuries. In the 16th century the Thum married a princess from Baltistan who brought master Balti craftsmen to renovate the building as part of her dowry. The architectural style is a clear indication of Tibetan influence in Baltistan at the time. In those days the Ultar Glacier was close enough to provide an icehouse at the back of the fort. It was indispensible for providing cold drinks, preserving food, and supplying the necessary cool air system throughout the fort during the hot daytime. The Mirs of Hunza abandoned the fort in 1945, and moved to a new palace down the hill. It, also, is in a strategic position looking up and down the valley.

Neither of us was very hungry, we were sick of rice and chicken and ordered omelettes for lunch the following day. We were drinking lots – water that is – to try and stave off the headaches. We had a great afternoon climbing the steep, dusty path to the bazaar and spent hours shopping. I bought a star ruby ring from a jeweller's shop, and some lapis lazuli. It's funny they didn't have garnet rings; maybe this stone is too common to bother with. After all as we had been able to gather them among the grit on the side of the road earlier, they can't be thought of as being very valuable. The shops were full of all sorts of semi-precious stones and carved wooden objects. Also, beautiful shawls, jackets and all manner of embroidered wall hangings and cushion covers in bright coloured silks and wools. And, of course, carpets. Everything was really lovely. One could happily give house-room to a lot of this beautiful craft work without spending a fortune. All the shopkeepers were so friendly, they seemed not to mind if you just looked and admired without buying. Yet again some of them invited us to join them for tea. On the way back down the path we got chatting to an ancient old guy sitting outside his house, who told us some weird tales of the locals and the British. He was either a bit doting or 'on' something but in any case we couldn't really understand what he was trying to tell us and we nodded and smiled before moving on.

By the evening the sky had totally cleared and there was a perfect new moon and we hoped for a fine day on the morrow. Some local musicians and dancers again performed for us later, all male and quite good, but for entertainment value, not a patch on the polo game. Our bedroom was, as usual, a disaster zone. I suppose the only tidy way to travel is not to carry any change of clothes, chemists bags, guidebooks or booze, and certainly to resist buying any souvenirs.

The PTDC Hotel at Sust was pretty horrible – and so was Sust, just a collection of grotty border stalls, cars, lorries, stones, dust and men. However, we had had a very interesting day getting here. Up in the morning at 7 am, we arrived at the Hoper glacier by 8 am in a borrowed jeep, as once again the road was too dicey for our minibus. Having crossed a slim suspension bridge, we arrived at a place above the glacier with a great view looking down and across it. The glacier is nearly 5,000 m/3-4 mi across and is dirty and gravely, but with huge clear spikes of ice rearing up from it, the complete antithesis of the pristine glaciers in Chile. The Hoper Glacier, which has a length of 58 km/36 mi, squeezes between two rock walls as it gradually grinds its way downhill. We had two or three boys with us offering to take us down a very rough track right on to the glacier. We had never been so close to one before, even in South America, and decided, despite Yousef's dire warnings, that we simply had to get right on to it. The pistol-cracks and groans from the glacier were eerily dramatic. Every so often we would jump at what sounded like loud thunder, which seemed to totally envelope us. It was, of course the shifting and cracking of the glacier, as we slipped and slithered down the steep slope and stepped gingerly onto the ice. Naturally enough we couldn't go much further than the edge, but it was worth it just to be there and wonder at the constant scouring away of the rock as the great river of ice gouged its interminable way down.

The track up to and down from the glacier winds through several villages with fruit trees and cropped fields. In one place there was a girl dressed in a purple gown up a tree picking apricots. It was such a pretty picture and so frustrating not to be able to photograph it. We walked quite a bit of the way down to be joined by some boys offering us hashish. Indian hemp grows everywhere here, commonly used to fence off the fields!

Having returned to the jeep for a few miles, it suddenly and unexpectedly broke down, right under a huge overhang. Elise and I immediately decided to start walking until we could hitch a lift. Yousef, unamused, was furious with the whole world in general.

"This is totally out of order," he raged.

"I'm sure it's not all that serious," Elise said, trying to console him. "We'll walk on and try and hitch a lift."

Oh dear. Not the right thing to say.

"You cannot possibly do that. You never know what might happen."

What *did* happen was that we walked off down the road. After a mile or so, we decided to sit down and wait for someone to come. Within a few minutes, a pick-up stopped and a kind and rather surprised driver offered us a lift. We happily hopped into the back and arrived, albeit a bit dusty, where we had planned to meet up with Yousef. All his fears were allayed.

Yousef was really terribly grumpy in the mornings. He wouldn't eat breakfast, so obviously his gargantuan lunches and dinners cheered him up as he was a different person in the evenings. He continued to treat us like children – "don't go near the edge," "don't walk in the middle of the road," and so on. He had told us at least three times to pack our bags before lunch. I started to answer him back, but possibly fortunately he interrupted me to speak to the driver, and so saved us both from a probable slanging match. Then, unexpectedly, he would go and do something great, like taking us to local restaurants or organizing the polo match.

The Kunjerab Pass
Off in the afternoon towards Sust, past an old ruby mine, and towards the, by now close, high black peaks of the Karakorum Range. We had to crawl over four cleared but huge, mucky land slides. It was all so dangerous, especially here where it was becoming steeper and steeper. During the drive Elise quietly said she had an admission to make.

"Go for it," I said and she replied

"I'll be very glad when we get over the pass and off the KKH." It was funny as I'd been thinking exactly the same thing.

North of Gulmit, which we walked through, the scenery became more and more barren. '*The scenery is stern and impressive, but too gloomy to be really sublime*', wrote British explorer Reginald Schomberg in 1935. Black mountains with razor-edged summits and bare, black walls drop sheer to the river and there was a fierce cold wind. Someone with a steady hand and a head for heights had climbed high up the scree slope and written messages such as 'welcome to Hussaini' in white paint on the rock-face. There was still electricity all the way along the KKH. How they maintain the poles I do not know, many of them are leaning at all sorts of odd angles, and often the wires are lying in great loops like Christmas-tree decorations. We passed the Passu and Batura glaciers, both within walking distance from the road. In fact the Batura, some years ago, at 62 km/38.5 mi long, came right to the road and crunched to smithereens the Chinese-built bridge – you can still see it. The glaciers progress and retreat depending on the temperature and snowfall.

I had a rather ropy tummy so had a comforting Cup-a-Soup and biscuit for dinner, which Elise said was horrible and even Yousef lacked his normal voracious appetite and pushed his meal around the plate. It became a horrible black night with pouring rain as we went to bed at 9.15. It wasn't a promising outlook for this crossing of the Kunjerab Pass the following day, where there had already been a huge wet landslide and reports of it being uncrossable.

I spent the night half awake, half asleep, when one's imagination runs riot, and I couldn't be sure if I was dreaming or awake. My nightmares of pouring rain, mud slides and the hotel being washed away – and us with it – were extremely disturbing. However, when the daylight came, it brought sunshine and a bright blue sky – what a relief. We went through the Pakistani customs in Sust and met our new driver in a government jeep for the trip up to and over the Kunjerab Pass. We said our fond farewells to Yousef and Fridoun. Suddenly they seemed like old friends, even though it was rather a love/hate relationship with Yousef, and we were sorry to see them go. We had had nothing but total kindness, friendship and good manners from everyone we met in Pakistan.

We had been reassured that the big landslide that had stopped all cross-border traffic for weeks had been cleared and we proceeded past the area where it had occurred and marvelled that it was possible to make the road passable again – the rock walls all seemed so insubstantial, how there are not more accidents we didn't know. Maybe there are but we just hadn't been told.

By now we were going up the narrow gorge of the Kunjerab River. Stopping at Dhee for immigration we drove through a stream that had burst its banks and on into the Kunjerab Nature Reserve. High up in the Karakoram chain a couple of thousand

Wakhi people reside among some of Pakistan's most spectacular and rugged mountain scenery. They scratch a living from combining animal husbandry with some work-migration and recently, trekking eco-tourism. Animals are moved over great distances utilizing pastures often many miles apart. Women take care of the yaks, sheep and goats on the summer pastures and the men take on the hard job of looking after the animals through the winter. Whereas the resident Wakhi-population has not been the source of great interest, conservation agencies have been made aware of the biodiversity importance of this area and its exceptional range of wild animals, some of them critically endangered. Apparently the area is home to the world's largest snow leopard population as well as the Himalayan brown bear, and wild ungulates such as blue sheep and Siberian ibex. The river up here is narrow, rushing, sparkling and blue now that it is no longer full of glacial moraine. We crossed the huge rock fall, which we had heard about days previously and which had since been encompassed into a very rough part of the road, and stopped to give a lift to a local workman. The road becomes much narrower (if that's possible) and starts a series of hairpin bends which is the beginning of the pass.

The pass itself lies in a bleak, stoney, shallow bowl at an altitude of a breathless 4,695 m/15,528 ft and at this point is the highest public highway in the world. Kunjerab means 'blood valley' in Tajik, presumably because of the numerous bandits who operated here during the Silk Road days. In bad weather it must be a terrible place to traverse. Even that day it was icy cold in the shade, but luck was with us and the sun shone from a cloudless sky. Some Chinese were crossing from China and we had to do a photo shoot with them. It was quite a laugh, each one wanted to be in a photo with us so we had to keep posing for about 6 photos taken in all. I think they were fascinated at meeting two somewhat curious, English-speaking ladies so far from home.

Kyhber Pass – Pakistan

Juncture of three great mountain ranges. L to R Hindu
Kush, Karakorum Range, Himalayas

Baltit fort
near
Karimabad –
Hunza Valley

Market –
Peshawar

XINJIANG REGION, CHINA
1998

I found you
folded in the armpit of a megadune.
you were crying,
and the winds of the Taklamaken Desert
whipped up sand –
it clung to your face.

I had been left by my Bactrian mate,
not long ago,
for a Uighur man with dusty black hair
and green eyes of jade.

Odawni AJ Palmer, 1979 –

The Glories of Tashkurgan

Down we slid into a smooth valley. The total antithesis from the south side of the pass. There was some road maintenance going on, so we had to wait quite a time, giving us an opportunity to watch lots of marmots scurrying around squealing. Sometimes lying in the sun or standing up keeping watch – quaint, rather attractive little creatures. A new river, tiny in its infancy, was running with us now, still with snow-capped mountains on either side. Horses, cattle, yaks, sheep, goats and Bactrian camels grazed contentedly across the wide green valley. A little family on camels and donkeys posed happily for our cameras. The bulk of the snowy Muztagh Ata loomed ahead of us.

The road went straight downhill – literally. It was quite a relief to be out of the almost claustrophobic, sheer heights of the

Pakistan KKH – we are obviously County Down Drumlin people at heart! It was all such an experience. And what a lesson in geology. We had been through some of the most massive, beautiful, but daunting scenery and met with some of the kindest people. But I'd never do it again – it was much too scary. We had a delightful picnic lunch (bless Yousef) beside the river, with the High Pamirs facing us, before continuing on towards Tashkurgan.

Customs and immigration were amazingly quick and we went on to meet our new guide, Abdul, a Uyghur from Kashgar. The Uyghur Turks came to western China about 750AD, and although when in 1955 the communists declared Xinjiang an autonomous region, it would never know anything of the sort. Although the Uyghurs outnumber the Han Chinese, friction has continued with the Chinese, including riots in the 1970s. An armed uprising by Muslim nationalists in October 1981 that may have left hundreds dead, was followed by another in 1990 and more recently in 2009. In each case scores of protestors were said to have been killed by government troops. It goes without saying, therefore, that the Muslim Uyghurs are keen to let you know right from the start that they are not Chinese and Abdul also made this abundantly clear.

Although quite an important town during the Silk Road days, Tashkurgan was now a most unprepossessing place. Our hostelry for the night was the Pamir Hotel, the roughest yet but although soulless, it was clean. We made ourselves a cup of tea, but it wasn't very hot. I recalled the physical geography lessons at school explaining to us about boiling point at altitude being so much lower than at sea level, and here we were so high up that boiling point was very low. Isn't education a wonderful thing? There was hot water available for two hours so we both had baths – what an unexpected luxury in the crazy free-standing bathroom. Nothing was attached, the basin you could pick up and run away with. The bath wobbled alarmingly when you got into it and the plumbing and electrics were a Chinese puzzle of pipes and wires all open and all over the place. Our guide book said 'food is a misery here and only provides for tour groups'. We wondered, did a group of two count?

To continue with our explorations, we went to see the ruins of a mud-brick fort, estimated to be about 600 years old, although local lore says Tashkurgan – which means stone fortress – has been a citadel for over 2300 years. Most of the fort's multilayered walls are still intact, and we were able to climb up on to them. It is most dramatic, and well worth a visit, especially as we saw it at the end of the day when the light was rosy touching the ancient ruins with a soft warmth and turning the snow to fire on the distant mountains. We walked through the farm area; tiny stone houses, and people busy with livestock. Some men were piling pea plants onto a trailer for cattle fodder. The little pods were still fresh and intact so we tried some. They were delicious, just like very young mangetout. On the outskirts of Tashkurgan we visited a Tajik cemetery where many of the head stones are portrayed as the Tajik or nomadic type of saddle, rather touching as a tribute to these nomadic people.

Our evening meal looked appalling, just as the book said, so we resorted to vodka, Mars bars and biscuits. Were we getting too old for these hostelries? We didn't know it then, but we hadn't even begun.

Muztagh Ata was very dramatic, its symmetrical shape glistening whiter than white in the early morning sunshine. We drove round it and viewed the Subash Hills and Mount Kongur, arriving at Lake Karakol in time for lunch. This is one of the most beautiful places imaginable. It was totally calm with the mountains opposite reflected upside down on the still water. There were lots of ducks and high above us eagles hung motionless on the warm thermals. Camels and donkeys grazed and we took a long walk along the water's edge. There were some visitors' yurts, which looked really nice but on talking to some Italians who had been trekking, they revealed that it was terribly cold at night, and as often happens when the weather closes in it could be pretty uncomfortable.

We continued on down the green valley with the River Ghez on our right side, into a shallow wet plateau surrounded, to our surprise, by enormous sand dunes. We stopped and Abdul introduced us to a young Kyrgis man. They had quite a chat and we discovered he was a nomadic shepherd, travelling miles throughout the summer keeping his hundred or so sheep and goats grazed. He wore ragged trousers and jacket and, as very common here, a flat cap. He had a gentle smile in a long narrow rather flat brown face and smelled of animals, sour milk and wood smoke. His sheep dog was more for warning him of wolves than herding the animals. He had some small, carved, wooden animals and old coins for sale, which he held out for us on his care-worn brown hands. God, what a hard life.

The roadway had become steeper again, and continued down through an area of constant rock falls, with the road completely disappearing from time to time as we picked our way over the rubble. At one point a bulldozer was clearing a passage. We walked through the stones and dirt, and discovered under the stones soft, sinking sand with constantly running water – no wonder the land is constantly on the move. We passed a lorry well and truly stuck, and two lorries full of horses bound for Pakistan – poor things, what a journey and what a dismal future for them. It doesn't do to brood on this sort of thing. We had to remind ourselves that one is only here as an observer and to try not to be censorial or emotional – but it's hard. Through a police stop where we bought delicious, hot, filled pastry pancakes. Although still feeling very well but not very hungry, we thoroughly enjoyed this little snack.

Kashgar's Magic Market.
We drove through a dramatic area of deep red rock full of mineral deposits. After two days of driving downhill, quite suddenly the

mountains on either side of us disappeared and we were on a flat plain. We could see the distant Tien Shan Mountains to the north in front of us and the vastness of the Taklamakan desert stretching to the horizon to the east on our right. Poplar trees lined the sides of the road and fields were cropped or grazed. As we neared the village of Upal the traffic became quite busy; not many cars, but plenty of pony and donkey carts jostling for position along the road. We stopped at Upal for a slimmer's lunch of beer and water melon and continued on into Kashgar - further away from the sea than any other city in the world. The Semen Hotel was our destination here. It used to be the Russian consulate and home from 1882 for many years of The Great Game, to the clever and manipulative Russian consul – Petrovsky. The hotel seemed very good and almost luxurious in comparison to the previous couple of nights. We had a nice room and showers and were able to do our hair and lots of clothes washing. After my little hiccup in Pakistan, we were both, amazingly, still feeling very well.

After an unexpectedly horrible meal we enjoyed a musical evening at the famous old British Embassy, then known as Chini Bagh, once the home of the British Consul, Sir George Macartney and his wife Catherine. Macartney was half Chinese, this fact being glossed over, since it was extremely rare in the 1800s to have a man of mixed parentage in the Foreign Office. They lived here for 28 years. On several occasions, with incredible bravado, they made the journey back to Britain crossing the mountain ranges on horse-back. Once an elegant bungalow with beautiful gardens, the consulate was now a sad, broken old wreck. But it was a greatly entertaining evening with a marvellous band playing various indigenous stringed instruments, and beautiful girls singing and dancing in national costume.

The famous Sunday market certainly lived up to its reputation. You could buy anything from a camel to a bicycle bell. And the people! Such faces. A photographer's dream. My bloody camera chose this minute to pack up and you just wanted to snap and snap continuously. Mountains of water melons, piles of exotic-smelling spices, heaps of fresh fruit and vegetables. On to the animal market. *Packed*. Horses being tried out, both ridden and 'in the hand'. Lines of various coloured donkeys waiting patiently. Hundreds of camels, goats and sheep, (some with the most rude-looking bums). Dust whirling. Men crying 'boish, boish' which sounds like 'push push', which means exactly that – 'make way'. Mountains of materials, quantities of galvanized buckets and other hardware items. Stalls full of jewellery, stalls full of all sorts of headgear, including some wonderful fur hats. Carts, bikes, baby's cradles with holes in the middle with little catheters for them to pee through, (how sensible, no wet nappies).Crowds of people in every sort of dress, men always in hats or caps, often with their trouser-flies open – funny the things you notice. Ladies at their stalls, mostly in long, bright cotton dresses sitting akimbo with wads of money stuffed down their stockings or in their bosoms. Lots of barbers' stands with queues of both bearded but bald, and hirsute customers awaiting the approach of the 'cut-throat'. Fantastic food stalls, offering unrecognizable and almost unmentionable pieces of animal, including sheep's balls, which are considered great delicacies. Great skeins of noodles and huge woks of rice, all smelling simply delicious. So much noise and excitement. We were so busy watching that we almost forgot to do any shopping. My meagre purchases amounted to a little packet of saffron and two small speakers for my walkman.

We had lunch with an Australian couple who we had met the night before. I had heard them talking and thought the man sounded Northern Irish. Indeed, what a coincidence as he was originally from Co Down. His wife was half Chinese and half Burmese, both, delightful people.

In the afternoon we went to see the Abakh Hoja Tomb. A really elegant small mausoleum built in the mid 1600s. With its brightly tiled dome and 4 minarets, it resembles a miniature Taj Mahal. Behind it is a vast graveyard with geometrically designed tombs long and conical all facing Mecca, and made of mud and chopped straw. We watched some workmen taking orders from an old boy who was meticulously organising and designing his own tomb.

Near the Id Kah mosque there is an interesting area full of Uyghur shops and narrow passages with adobe houses that seemed to have come from a time long past. There are streets of blacksmiths, farriers, wood carvers, carpenters, jewellers, potters, metal knife and tool makers. We spent ages watching these artisans working away, wonderful to see men still able to work with their hands like this. It's sad that we have lost so many of these skills back home. Another street was all tailors with sewing machines rattling away. Shoe makers, bicycle menders and lots of shops selling all sort of tobacco, much of which is grown nearby.

We ate at John's Café that evening, not far from the hotel. It was quite a spot for travellers and we joined four young people for a good meal and had fun swapping 'traveller's tales', noticing all the time that we were probably light years older than anyone else in the place. Then, to our utmost amazement, in desert dry Kashgar, where we understood it *never* rained, the heavens opened to a downpour of lashing rain, crashing thunder – and yes, flashing lightening, and we found ourselves having to dive back through the torrent to the cover of our hotel.

After the night's heavy rain the morning was dull – the city wet and muddy. We were off today to tackle the Torugart Pass to enter Kyrgistan, giving a lift to a friend of Abdul who lived in the same village of Artush. When we arrived in Artush we asked Abdul if we might go and visit his home and maybe meet his family. He was delighted and so were we. His house was one of several in the same family compound. Green and shady outside, the houses were adobe and very, very simple. One room on two levels served as sitting room and bedroom. Woven hangings decorated the walls and mats and cushions covered the raised area, with rush mats on the floor. We were served with tea and very sweet sort of biscuits, by Abdul's aunt, flashing a valuable set of gold teeth. The family were shy but curious and we kept having to ask them to join us on the 'bed' and to drink the tea.

We spent the longest time yet going through customs, filling in forms and being scrutinised by officers. We met three Englishmen who had already spent two whole days battling with red tape. They were on a long expedition, unaccompanied and hoping to bring their Landrover over the border. We wished them well and eventually we went through. Not a smile anywhere from anyone.

It soon started raining again and as we progressed upwards the road became very wet with water running down across our road from the mountains. It was only a matter of time before we were stopped by a river in spate cascading across the road, over the bridge that it should have gone under. We all decided it looked too dangerous to cross and while the two men worked out the best plan Elise and I put on our macs and went for a purposeful walk. While we were some way away we saw a pickup approaching and without hesitation it whooshed through the torrent. The van stopped and two men got out and encouraged our guys through. We shot down the hill, jumped into the car and gritting our teeth, set off across the wild tumbling water. Wow, quite nerve-wracking, and we thought we had passed all the hazards!

Landslide. Karakorum Highway

Bread seller Kashgar market

Near lake
Karakol

Tajik cemetery –
Tashkurgan

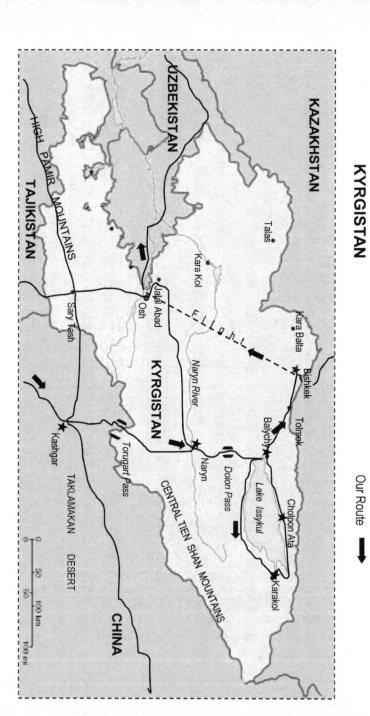

KYRGISTAN

Our Route ➡

KYRGISTAN

1998

A bright moon rising above the Tian Shan Mountains,
Lost in a vast ocean of clouds.
The long wind, across thousands and thousands of miles,
Blows past the Jade-gate Pass.

Li Bai, 701 – 762

The Torugart Pass and Round Lake Issyk-Kul

Gradually, as we ascended, the rain became sleet and we could see the softer, rounder heights of the Tian Shan Mountains covered in snow. We passed through a checkpoint with ghastly abandoned Chinese buildings half falling down. Here, we were interrogated by about ten Chinese whose opening shot was how old were we? We lied. Shortly after we arrived at the bleak border on the 3,657 m/12,000 ft Torugart Pass at 1 pm.

There was nobody there to meet us so we just had to wait rather anxiously in the car, watching the snow falling from a slate-grey sky. By 2 pm, then snowing very heavily, we had still seen no sign of any transport to meet us and Elise was convinced we had been forgotten. Eventually at 2.30 pm a bus appeared out of the blizzard, from Kyrgistan, with 29 American, Jules Verne travellers on board. They disgorged themselves looking cold, miserable and somewhat bemused dragging coats and bags out into the snow.

There was a certain amount of doubt from Abdul as to whether this was *our* transport – a whole bus to ourselves? But, having shuffled through the deepening show, in we got, and away, with a Russian driver and a very large, cheerful lady, the guide to the departed Americans. She produced a beautiful packed lunch left over from the previous occupants and like a couple of happy hamsters we tucked in to cold chicken, hard-boiled eggs and salad and stocked up the rucksacks with tomatoes and cucumbers. Oh what it is to be wealthy, cosseted Americans.

We had to show our passports to border police continually, then down, out from the snowy wastes into a landscape of beautiful, sun-dappled, green steppe. Herds of horses and horsemen were everywhere. A beautiful, perfect rainbow added the finishing touch to the already enchanting scene. I wondered, would we each find a pot of gold at the ends of the rainbow?

After a five-hour drive we arrived at Naryn and a yurt camp for the night. They were pretty primitive conditions but we thoroughly enjoyed a great meal in a communal building, and our lady from the bus becoming more jolly by the minute introduced us to Kara Balta, the Kyrgis vodka that was to be our refreshment until the end of our journey.

We spent a freezing cold night in the yurt. However we piled on all the clothes we had with us in order to keep Jack Frost at bay. Up until now we had had a mix of western-type lavatories and the hunker-down type. Here though, it was definitely a rather grotty squatter! A dog barked from time to time during the night, which woke us both. Mostly the beds were pretty uncomfortable, but I had become accustomed to not sleeping well and just made up for it during the day in the car, which was annoying as I missed bits of scenery. Not surprisingly, Elise always wondered how I could possibly go to sleep during dramatic drives. So did I. The morning was beautiful and sparkly again, so welcome after the rain and snow of the previous day.

On we went, still going downhill on our way towards Lake Issyk-Kul, over the Dolon Pass at a mere 3,000 m/9,100 ft. We had yesterday's bus driver Victor and a new young translator called Olga, both fair-haired and obviously Russian. We had no idea where we were going. Our itinerary said overnight in yurts for two nights, but theirs said Lake Issyk-Kul two nights and we discovered we were going to the town of Karakol at the eastern end of the lake, to a hotel. This flat agricultural land certainly wasn't the Kyrgistan we had hoped to experience. We were both disappointed as we had very much wanted to stay in the High Pamirs with the nomadic herders and possibly go and see eagle-hunting. Anyway there was nothing we could really do about it and comforted ourselves with the thought that everything you experience is a learning curve. We set off down the Bishkek road watching everyone going to work on horseback, wearing traditional high white felt hats.

The scenery here was quite bland except for the brilliant blue lake which, lying at an altitude of nearly 2,773 m/5,000 ft above sea level, is said to be the world's second largest alpine lake after Lake Titicaca in Peru. A combination of extreme depth, thermal activity and mild salinity means the lake never freezes. Its moderating effect on the climate, plus an abundant rainfall at it's east end, have made it somewhat of a venue for travellers throughout the ages. This whole area was off limits to foreigners in Soviet times and not a bit of wonder, as Olga hinted that there were, officially sanctioned, plantations of opium poppies and cannabis around the lake. More importantly Issyk-Kul was used by the Soviet navy to test high precision torpedoes far away from inquisitive eyes.

Elise and I needed no persuading when Olga asked would we like to go for a bathe in Lake Issyk-Kul. Neither she nor we had cozzies so we asked – no, told – Victor to go for a walk. With nobody else about, in we went. We found the water amazingly warm after the cold of the previous day.

There was no traffic as we continued on along a good road. No people, bar odd farm workers bringing in hay and several horsemen going about their business. The land gradually became very pastoral between the lake and the mountains with small, Ukrainian-looking villages built by the Russians at the turn of the century. A very odd mix of peoples here, the Kyrgis who are predominately nomadic horsemen, a lot of Russian settlers and a few Dungan Chinese.

We arrived in Karakol and had a late lunch, after which we went to see the pretty Russian Orthodox Holy Trinity Cathedral. It was completed in 1890 after the original stone building fell down in an earthquake. As we entered the garden, we were greeted by the evocative perfume of old-fashioned roses. The church was a nice old wooden building badly needing paint, looked after by an elderly man with an intelligent, interesting face and grey hair in a pony tail. His chequered career included being a sailor and a journalist. Having become disenchanted with life and the changes in politics he had become a bit of a recluse taking a great pride in his church and lovely rose garden.

In the late afternoon we took ourselves off for an exploration of Karakol. It seemed to be a peaceful town full of small, wooden houses, surrounded by apple orchards. Our perambulations brought us to a large arena with a grandstand and deduced it was for horse racing, discovering later that this was Central Asia's first hippodrome. We walked on and came across stables with three or four men at work with the horses. We had absolutely no common language but they were all so friendly and beckoned us in to see the horses. On an off chance I hazarded a guess and said "Akhal-Teke" which I knew was a breed of horse similar to the Arab and which came from Central Asia. The man immediately understood and said "niet, New Kyrgis." Presumably a breed of horse. He beckoned to us to follow him to his car and said "hotel". As we both happily climbed in I reminded Elise that our mummies had always told us never to take lifts with strangers! Our new friend took us back to our hotel and indicated that he would be back.

Right enough in about half an hour he returned with a young interpreter and we had a wonderful hour's chat about horses, and he certainly knew all about the Akhal-Teke. They told us there was a 'horse factory' on the other side of the lake, which we might visit. His phrase very much amused us, but we deduced – and hoped – it would probably be a stud farm rather than a horse meat factory. We found that in the Hippodrome, on Independence Day there is a great celebration with all sorts of horse riding, racing and games, one of which is a game called *Ulak-Tartysh*. This is something that we would have to see. The Steppe people are all skilled riders, able to grab a calf or goat from the ground while riding a horse at full gallop. A goal is scored when a player gets the goat or calf clear of the other players and tosses it across the goal line. The game is also known as *Buztashi* in other central Asian countries. It is popular with the Afghans, Uzbeks, Kazaks, Turkmans and Tajiks. It sounded tremendous fun and what a bit of luck to have fallen in with this guy who turned out to be the local director of tourism and sport.

Nikolai Przhevalsky, the Russian explorer died here from typhus in 1888 from drinking water from the near-by Chuy River while hunting tiger. A huge memorial of an eagle on top of a sculpted plynth of granite has been erected in his memory. From here we could see the lake with two grey cutters moored – the sum total of the Kyrgis navy. The small Prezhevalsk Museum itself is well-worth visiting, featuring a huge map of Przhevalsky's explorations and a gallery of exhibits on his life – including a stuffed specimen of the wild horse – with some of the information in English. During his career Przhevalsk conducted expeditions through Siberia, Mongolia, Central Asia and China. But his name mainly survives today in the Przhevalsky horse, a miniature wild species that he found in Mongolia. It became extinct in the wild in the 1960s, but survived in captivity, and has recently been reintroduced into its natural habitat.

About lunchtime we stopped on the north shore of Lake Issyk-Kul to have another swim. After a long walk we enjoyed a picnic of lots of lovely fresh bread, sausages, cheeses and fruit, and a wonderful local thick clotted cream called *kaimak*, all bought previously in Karakol market. The lake is very shallow on this side and we had to wade in miles before it was deep enough to swim.

On then along the lake shore to the Issyk-Kul Sanatorium. Well, these two days were not really what we had expected. We thought we would be two nights in yurts, mountain-walking and finding horse-riding nomads, instead of which we now found ourselves in this extraordinary old relic of Soviet times. It was an enormous sanatorium with extensive, laid out grounds reaching to the lake. The view from all the rooms was wonderful, over the lake to the Tian Shan Mountains. Our room, amazingly, had a working fridge – yippee! But as usual, the loo was awful, no top on the cistern, no seat and no handle you had to plunge your hand into the cistern and push down the ball-cock. There were miles of corridors on five floors but only about 20 rooms in use. It was enormous and concrete-grey, and terribly depressing. We found it eerie, full of ghosts, and reeking of the old Soviet Union but it was today, and independence is here, and nobody now can afford to come to these relics of a bygone age. It was a short walk down through the gardens to a sandy beach for swimming. The gardens were neglected, the pools had no water, the fountains didn't work and the flowerbeds were almost bereft of flowers.

However, when we got to the beach we discovered some sort of a party going on. A couple of men came over to us and asked us to join them and some Swiss for tea. Not known to refuse an invitation, off we went and found a hell of a party going on with everybody in absolutely cracking form and offering vodka rather than tea! Songs were sung to a guitar and lots of toasting each other's health. It eventually transpired that the Swiss were representatives of Siemens. They had been trying to set up business with some Russians and Kazaks in Almaty, but had found too many difficulties and red tape. In the end some of the Russians had suggested a party on Lake Issy Kul as an informal get-together and thank-you to the Swiss and had come here by boat for the day. We had such a laugh with them all and then the Swiss guitarist started singing to me the old 1950s Paul Anka song 'Oh Please Stay by Me, Diana' and as he couldn't think of a song with the name Elise in it, had the brilliant idea of singing 'Oh Champs Elysee' as a tribute to Elise.

If you have never experienced a seriously awful breakfast, then this was the place to have one. Consisting of three courses of stuffed eggs, which weren't bad, repulsive meatballs and mash, and an even more repulsive looking pud which brave Elise said was rice pudding. It might have been OK, but cold leftovers from dinner the night before for breakfast, I could not even contemplate. It's actually very funny in hind-sight. The previous night we were brought a menu but,

a) it was in Russian and Kyrgis, and

b) we had no idea that we were supposed to choose our breakfast from it for the following day.

Well, I mean to say – how were we supposed to know?Some other visitors with a smattering of English had tried to explain to us. But our powers of deduction had escaped us and it wasn't until we were leaving that we discovered that we could in fact possibly have had something rather better to eat – too late, too late!

Around Lake Issyk Kul is far more Russian than Kyrgis. It's a sort of geo-physical time warp, with horses everywhere, being ridden and driven, all the hay carts and many small personal carts pulled by horses or donkeys. There were almost no tractors or cars, no buses or lorries, but quite good roads. Often along the road we saw children keeping the verges tidy. We stopped at the stud we had been told about in Karakol. This was a massive place with stabling for 200 horses. Swallows flew in and out of broken windows, long grass and weeds grew everywhere, and broken and cracked doors contained the 40 or so inmates. We met the head man and some of his stable lads who obviously cared deeply for the horses who, although a bit thin seemed kind and mannerly. The pride of the yard was a pure bred Akhal-Teke stallion, a gift from the President of Kazakstan to the President of Kyrgistan. The breed is naturally fine-boned and long-backed, but this one had a really bad 'parrot mouth', that is, a very over-pronounced upper jaw. We wondered if the president knew that this was a bad inheritable fault. These horses are not suited to damp but flourish in the deserts of Turkmenistan and can go on for huge distances in hot, dry conditions. We were invited to go riding, but as we had already organized this activity later on, very politely declined. It was, however, a real bonus for us to see these horses, a very, very lucky chance.

Bishkek and a Flight to Osh
At the west end of the lake the land was much dryer and hotter. We drove to Bishkek through the mountains beside the Chuy River, (making sure not to try the water) which divides Kyrgistan from Kazakstan. Olga was very sick on the side of the road, (did she eat the terrible breakfast, or drink the Chuy water?) So instead of going to the museum in the afternoon, we went off to explore the town. We thought we were going towards the centre, but Olga had given us wrong directions, not our fault this time – and although we had a map we had started from the wrong place – very Irish – and we ended up in Ala-Too Square instead of TSUM, the big department store. Anyway we were able to buy *cold* juice and water.

The population of Bishkek is multi-racial, only about one third being Kyrgis. It's quite pretty with lots of trees and no high rise buildings, wide streets and Ukrainian style houses, but everything seemed to be rather lifeless. Ala Too Square, we thought, was attractive with fountains playing and a few quiet folk enjoying the sun. However, there are two huge and elegant shop facades with columns and decorated windows hung with enormous banners looking very grand and rather Italian, but they are exactly that – just facades, hiding a knitwear factory! Extraordinary. Our hotel was situated on one of the broad and airy parks, but was dingy and empty, although we had a reasonable meal and everyone seemed friendly if somewhat curious. Here our loo was complete, and there was hot water, but the room was just plain drab: beige carpet, beige flowery walls, violent violet velvet curtains and beds with minimal sheets, just wide enough to cover the mattress. I mostly used my own sheet bag. In fact we had had *some* hot water everywhere we had been, and the rooms and beds had been clean so no real complaints, it was all just so colourless. Again and again we reassessed our values. Are, in fact, our Western values all wrong? Are we so spoiled with our consumer society? Does it matter one jot that it's all so colourless and that the toilets are falling apart and the food is pretty awful. I don't suppose anybody else even notices.

In the morning we went to the Museum of Fine Arts – it was open. We saw a terrific exhibition of art by local painters. So many differing styles, lots of it very, very good. The cut felt wall-hangings and carpets were wonderful. This was done by having different brilliantly coloured layers of felt stuck together. The design is drawn on the top layer and then cut down through the layers as far as the appropriate colour. It's very clever and they were really lovely. I thought I'd rather like to have a go at doing it some day. There was an expensive artefact shop, but not one postcard to be found. We continued on to the Lenin Museum, but although the doors were open, they refused to let us in. The doorman was quite angry and aggressive. It appeared that these workers never got paid and so sometimes they just dug their toes in and went on strike. I can't say I blame them. There have been anti-government street demonstrations about lack of pay in Bishkek in 2004, 2005 and 2006 – each time put down without too much bloodshed.

The Ala Archa Canyon is about 32 km/20 mi from Bishkek. There are several treks from the base, but we, guided now by the very fit and well – and *young* Olga - took off up the most demanding and dramatic, Ak Say canyon. The path climbs up steeply, high above the river, starting at about 2,133 m/7,000 ft. We were pathetic, stopping every few minutes to get our breath.

We seemed to have done better with our walks and climbs in Pakistan. Maybe the last week had been too sedentary and we had become soft! But it was wonderful scenery; high mountains, and loads of wild flowers. We had a picnic lunch on a high knoll, when, to my surprise, Elise decided to turn back – not like her at all. Olga and I staggered on (well I staggered on) determined to get to a waterfall. We made it eventually, after a couple of hours, and filled our water bottles from its icy water. I was really pleased as from there you could also see the Ak Say Glacier, shining blue and green across the canyon. What a perfect picture and wonderful to have a day out of the car. Going back down was even more hazardous than going up as it was so slippery, but we were back with Elise in no time, downhill all the way.

On our way to bed that night, we found the key-lady on our floor most insistent that we pull our curtains instead of prancing around for all to see. We thought we *had* drawn the curtains, but did as we were told and hopped into bed. Then, about 11pm we had a weird and most explicit phone call in broken English. Prostitution beckoned? But we thought better of it and battened down the hatches!

We thought we would go to the big supermarket TSUM in the morning, just to nosey around and see what was on offer. What do you know – it was closed. Yet again, staff hadn't been paid, so we went to a small supermarket instead to try our luck and see what was for sale. It was well stocked with Chinese clothes, Russian alcohol, and Kyrgis food.

The airport, about 19.3 km/12 mi from Bishkek, was from where we took one of our two internal flights. We said a fond farewell to Viktor who turned out to be a lovely man once he got to know us a bit. He was nothing like as stern and grim-faced as he had seemed when we first met him at the Kyrgis border. Olga stayed with us through security. She had been a great guide, very young but interested in us, and suggesting things to do to make our trip more pleasant.

So much for Kyrgistan. We did enjoy Lake Karakol although we didn't manage to learn much about the Kyrgis people – the only two we met to talk to were the shepherd in China and our nice director of tourism in Karakol. Now, looking back on it, tourism in 1998 was still in the hands of Russians and I presume they couldn't imagine a pair of ladies wanting to live like nomadic Kyrgis. So for reasons of their own, they took us instead, to an area, although interesting, was more Russian than Kyrgis. With both our driver and translator also being Russian, we found that most of the good jobs were still held by Russians, but that the state had run out of money so badly that nobody was being paid. Pensions were hardly worth the paper they were written on. The one big bonus was meeting up with the Akhal-Teke horse and the racing stable. We did, however, learn how to deal with disappointment and make the best of what was on offer. Poor food and awful bathrooms made our accommodation in Pakistan seem positively luxurious.

Our flight number was different from that of a party of Americans also waiting for the flight to Osh, but in fact we ended up on the same plane. There were no seat numbers so it became a great free-for-all as we staggered up into the tiny plane carrying our own luggage. The American group struggled on board clutching not only their bags, but sweaters, anoraks, one or two fur coats and walking sticks. One elderly American lady had an awful time juggling with quantities of baggage (one of the fur-coat brigade). She collapsed onto the seat next to me and said she was absolutely hating the whole trip and would not be leaving her hotel again (not even in Samarkand!) She had read all about it and as long as she could tell 'the folks back home' that she had been there, would not bother going to see this amazing place. Can you imagine that? Fancy coming this far and not going to see the very best bit.

None of us were greatly surprised to have no safety drill. The back of my chair coggled all over the place while the rest of the seats were more or less attached to the floor – a screw here and a screw there. This rickety old plane and the shocked discomfiture of the group of up-market Americans was so anachronistic that I wanted to laugh. I looked round at Elise who shrugged her shoulders and grinned ruefully. Despite it all, looking out of the window there were great views over the mountains. As we approached Osh, on the left-hand-side in front of us, I thought it must be the crinkled relief of The High Pamirs – the Roof of the World, and Tajikistan. Would we ever get there? I wondered.

Trekking in
the Ala
Archa
Canyon

Torugart Pass

Racing stables
– Karakol

View from the
road to Naryn

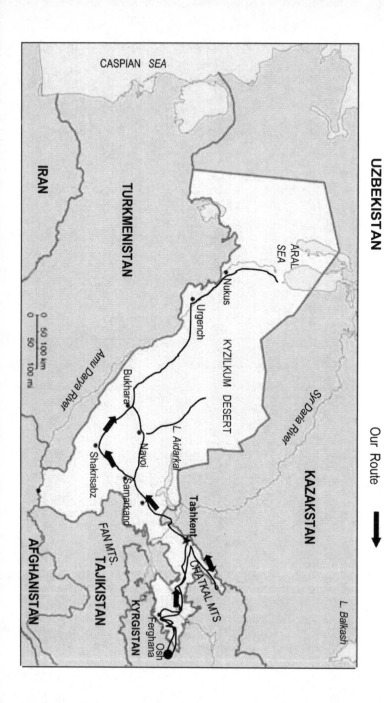

UZBEKISTAN

Our Route ➡

CASPIAN *SEA*

IRAN

TURKMENISTAN

ARAL SEA

Nukus

Urgench

KYZILKUM DESERT

Syr Darla River

Bukhara

Amu Darya River

L. Aidarkal

Navoi

Shakrisabz

Samarkand

Tashkent

KAZAKSTAN

L. Balkash

FAN MTS.

TAJIKISTAN

CHATKAL MTS

AFGHANISTAN

KYRGISTAN

Ferghana

Osh

0   50   100 km
0   50   100 mi

UZBEKISTAN
1998

We travel not for trafficking alone,
By hotter winds our fiery hearts are fanned,
For lust of knowing what may not be known
We take the golden road to Samarkand.

James Elroy Flecker, 1884 – 1915

The Doubtful Joys of Kara Balta and The Ferghana Valley.
We were met at Osh by a new guide and driver, Alexei and
Nikolai respectively. Off we went to Osh bazaar, reputed to be a
close second to Kashgar market, but in fact proving to be most
disappointing. There were endless stalls of cheap Chinese clothing
and rugs, however there were also bright pyramids of lovely fresh
local fruit and vegetables. We bought a watermelon and some
water, and as we were getting into the car Nikolai went off to buy
himself, a bottle of Kara Balta vodka, which we had originally
sampled in Naryn. It was here we learned that this is the best and
most desirable vodka so we bought a bottle also.

It was still hot. We hadn't seen a cloud now since crossing the
Torugurt Pass. Over the Kyrgis border and into Uzbekistan we
trundled, with no real problems, just more forms to fill in and a
declaration of how many dollars we had. We discovered when we
stopped at a fairly innocuous roadside café that women were not
allowed in. Second-class citizens? I don't think so. This wouldn't
do at all – we hoped that this was not a feature of things to come.
Anyway we continued along the road and stopped at a cotton
plantation and sat among the cotton plants to eat our watermelon

and have a long drink of water. This was our lunch, combined with an educational talk about cotton culture. The melons everywhere had been amazing. Watermelons. Huge oval ones like honeydew, and others like very large cantaloupe. They were for sale in markets and all along the roadside, built up into enormous pyramids. Also lining the roadside, for sale on rickety tables, were apples, pears, peaches and grapes.

Like many of the presidents in Central Asia, Islam Karimov was head of the republic's communist party until 1991 when, overnight, he reinvented himself as an Uzbek national patriot. But old habits die hard, and his tough line has earned Uzbekistan a very poor human rights record. Justifying himself against suspected terrorists he is reported to have said in the Uzbek parliament, "Such people must be shot in the head. If necessary, I will shoot them myself." What a delightful fellow.

The Ferghana Valley is very flat and totally cultivated, mostly with cotton (they are the world's second largest producer) but also wheat, maize and lots of vegetables. It's all very tidy. The roads are often lined with mulberry trees, the leaves of which are used for silk-worm culture. Agricultural irrigation, particularly for the thirsty cotton, is responsible for drying up the Amu Daria (Oxus), with the knock-on effect of the huge reduction in size of the Aral Sea. The mountains – not far away – were invisible, hidden behind a pall of vile yellow smoke from chemical plants.

The Zeirat Hotel had no hot water, but I felt so hot and sticky that I had a freezing shower and washed my hair before going out on the town. This time the bathroom was all complete albeit on a slope, so you emerged from the shower and slid downhill on the wet tiles towards the basin. Wouldn't it be great if it all came together just once?

Oh for God's sake, stop being such a grumpy old lady, Diana.

This proved to be a hilarious evening with Alexei, Nikolai and their chum, Fareed who wanted to practice his English. They took us to an outdoor restaurant with lots of very good food, lots of dancing and copious quantities of vodka. Every time someone wanted a drink there were toasts all round. Toasts to Ireland, Uzbekistan, Russia, women, men, love, you name it, we toasted it. We danced and drank the night away being pretty legless by the time we reeled back to the hotel. I certainly wasn't in any shape to write any diary that night, in fact never even managed to get undressed – oh my Lord!

Oh dear, oh dear, how are the mighty fallen. Elise was – or seemed – in fine fettle all the next day, but I was not just the best! As a rule, I don't get hangovers, but I did that time. Having groped my way out of bed and played with my breakfast, I made a sterling effort and joined the others at the car. The Sunday bazaar at Margilon was excellent. Masses and masses of beautiful fruit and veggies – three or four sorts of onions and yellow and orange carrots. Of course piles of brightly-coloured sweet-smelling spices and dried, powdered tomato. Jars of all sorts of different honey and freshly baked bread and cakes all smelling delicious. Almost totally Uzbek, the people had handsome smiling faces, all with acres of gold teeth.

Margilon has been in existence since about the first century BC and a key player in Central Asia's silk trade. A tall, gentle, handsome man welcomed us into his home of silk-weavers and told us all about dyeing and weaving the silk using some artificial dyes, others natural. I bought a long naturally dyed scarf. The whole of this Tajik family lived and worked together, two or three sons and two or three daughters, with wives, husbands and children. They served us tea and watermelon outside under a pergola dripping with ripe grapes.

A Group of Two!

Travelling on to Kuva – originally known as Quba in some tenth century Arabic texts – we saw where enormous excavations of a 4th to 7th century BC Buddhist temple is being tidied up and made fit for tourists. Having spent quite a long time exploring the large, dusty site we arrived back at the hotel hot and dirty and managed to persuade the management into giving us a big bucket of hot water for a good wash.

We spent a most amusing time at the hotel viewing other tourists, of which there were quite a few, surmising as to their nationality, number in group, where they had been and so on. The Swiss tour leader of some Americans who had obviously seen us watching them, asked if he could join us as he needed a little light relief from his somewhat difficult group. He wondered what tour *we* were with, and when we replied that we weren't with a tour, he was amazed and said,

"You are just a group of two then?"

Yes, we agreed, we were just a group of two. Nobody else was a group of two.

"But everybody travels in a big group here," he said.

"No," we replied, "not us. We always travel just the two of us."

"This is much better," said our new friend, "in a large group all you see are the other members of the party – not the country."

The groups varied from about nine to a large Japanese group of 35. As a group of two we certainly had seen more and got more information from local people and for sure a big group wouldn't have done the previous night's lark. Here was the first time we had seen so many tourists and of course they would increase as we approached Samarkand and Bukhara.

We ate very quietly with Alexei and Fareed. Alexei had been reasonably sober last night, taking his responsibilities more or less seriously. He *was* awfully serious and not at all a happy camper. He wanted to leave Uzbekistan. His parents were German, so he thought he would like to go to Germany as he was tall and fair and certainly didn't belong amongst the Uzbeks. But lack of money was a huge problem since the Soviet break-up. We heard this *everywhere*. Fareed was better off as he worked for an oil company where he earned the princely sum of $300 a month and just did the tour guide job to practice his English, the language most used, even for the Japanese. He was married with two children.

Fareed had had a very successful day with his group of 35 Japanese tourists. They had read about the famous 'Flying' or 'Celestial Horse' which sweated blood and which was, they thought, bred here in the Ferghana Valley many years ago. It was discovered around 114BC by Chang Ch'ien a commander in the guard of Emperor Wu-ti. The horse's qualities of beauty, size and stamina were not possessed by the Chinese indigenous breeds. So Chang Ch'ien brought a great many of them back to China to breed with the much heavier Chinese war horse. These Japanese visitors particularly wanted to see the descendants of this fabled animal, probably, in fact, the Akhal-Teke horse. Of course Fareed had no idea about this animal and eventually, using his initiative, stopped his bus at the roadside where he could see a farmer with his labouring horse ploughing a field, and said that indeed this was the horse they were asking about. The farmer was beckoned over and suddenly found himself the centre of attention with a bus load of tourists excitedly photographing him and his trusty steed from every angle. Well, good for Fareed. We all had a really good laugh at his story.

Nikolai was not with us that evening, we were told that he had to fix a sick car but perhaps it was Nik who was sick.

This whole area of Central Asia still produced a lot of silk and so the following morning we went to visit a silk factory in Marghilan. This time it was Alexei's turn to be sick, I don't know what these people are made of; not the stuff of Irish women anyway. I had felt awful, but at least I wasn't sick! I presumed, again stupidly, that a factory would mean somewhere with a fairish number of automated machines. But no. We were told about 300 were employed, but we saw nobody in the cocoon house (taking the thread from the cocoons in boiling water) – that's done in April and May. One guy 'carding', taking 50 threads from 50 bobbins and threading them together onto an enormous frame. Three men 'knotting', tying plastic and cotton thread tightly onto the undyed threads for dyeing according to the pattern. Four lads, including a 15-year-old 'casting-on' the fine, fine threads for the first knotted row of weaving, and five people weaving and four girls making carpets. That made 17 by my reckoning. Where were all the others? It was all unimaginably fine dexterous work. It only impinged on me eventually that, so far as I could make out, whereas with most weaving the warp is plain colour and the weft is what makes the pattern, with this it's the warp that has all the colour and pattern and the weft is a plain colour. I bought a length of brilliant gold/yellow shot with red, just enough to make two cushion covers.

For lunch we went to a *chai khana* (tea house) in Rishtan, where they allowed women. Hurray! We lounged outdoors on divans, watching, I have to say, men only, coming and going and playing chess, while plates of delicious pilaf (pronounced *plov*), kebabs and tea were brought to us. Here we were almost on the border with Tajikistan and many of the people have the Tajik characteristics, being of slight build and fine boned. Rishtan's potters are well known for their beautiful pots and bowls in mostly blue and green colours. Again, the potter we visited, was a Tajik with a strong intelligent face and beautiful hands.

The palace of the final Khan Khudoyar, in Kokand, shares a park with a dance hall and ping-pong tables. The palace is hugely ornate with ceramic tiles outside and carved and painted ceilings inside. Completed in 1873, it was then being restored. One small irony as we were led through this ornamentation, tucked into a gateway was a 20 ft high relief poster of a Russian soldier with a 'languishing' peasant in his arms gazing up at him, with the date 1941 inscribed above.

Having just crossed over the Syr Daria River we stopped for some of its huge trout-like fish. Fried at the side of the road, they were very tasty, but bony. Heading on for the Kamchik Pass we discovered the road was under construction. All day it had been hot and windy and with so much traffic and with all the dust stirred up there was practically no visibility as darkness fell. Literally dozens of broken down cars and vans littered the edges of the road, their drivers looking like topless bodies as they tinkered under the bonnets. The only other road in and out of the Ferghana Valley is through Tajikistan and that border was closed.

Tashkent and the 'Shoddy' Hotel.

We arrived at what we thought was the Shodlik Hotel in Tashkent about 8.30 pm. This time the permutation was as usual, dreary brown and beige colour scheme, not bad beds, hot water, complete loo, non-working air conditioning, and no fan but... *alive* with bugs. Ants, flies, tiny spiders and horror of horrors, cockroaches – really awful. We sprayed the room thoroughly and went down for drinks in the bar with Nick and Alexei. Poor Alexei was going on again about his situation: unmarried, and with no love for his present country. He talked again about leaving Uzbekistan and trying to go to either Germany or the Ukraine, but would they want him? Many Germans had arrived in Central Asia via a more forced route. As the Soviet-Union fought Nazi Germany in World War Two, many ethnic Germans were deported to Central Asia as a precaution against collaboration with the invading army. Alexei was probably the son of one of those deportees and now knew nobody in Germany. Like everyone else in these newly independent countries, he had no idea of sorting himself out, just kept waiting for 'the State' to fix it. He got quite a lot of employment in the summer translating, but the winters were very hard. Possibly if he could have really improved his English he might have got permanent work as a translator. He left us there in Tashkent to return to Ferghana, so we said farewell to tall, thin, sad Alexei. We were very sympathetic but really had no idea what it would be like to be in his situation. It must have been terrible to be brought up in the belief that communism was right, and the rest of the world was wrong, only to learn, virtually overnight, that what you had believed was, in fact, wrong. Or was it?

For the inhabitants of Tashkent and visitors like ourselves, one of the favourite places for recreation are the spurs of the Tian-Shan. A big mountainous area that stretches all along the territory of Central Asia for 1,200 km/745.6 mi from Peak Pobeda and Khan-Tengry in the east to the tops of Big Chimghan in the south-west. 80 km/49.7 mi from Tashkent, at the junction of three wild mountain rivers – the Ugham, Chatkal and Pskem – the high dam of Charvak Hydropower Station has been built, which has created a huge artificial lake, surrounded by green snow-topped mountain slopes. In this national preserve the mountain slopes are covered with relic spruce forests and in the valleys crossed by numerous rivers there are birch and walnut groves. We were up and away early, amazed to be woken by the alarm clock and not a bug in sight. Nikolai and a new guide called Zhenya called for us to go to the Chimghan Mountains to go riding. The scenery was splendid and we had active, sure-footed little horses. There was no proper saddle but a sort of metal tree with just mats and old bits of felt to sit on. We had stirrups but just an old rope for a bridle. Up we went accompanied by a chorus of birdsong through a gorge on very rough going, high steep mountain-sides around us. A herd of quite wild-looking horses, alerted by our scrabbling hoof-falls, came cantering over, very inquisitive as to our progress. Zhenya took it in turns with another lad to walk or ride. He was small and very attractive and moved like a dancer. I was fascinated by him.

We had finished our ride, tired and happy, and had stopped for a drink and yet more melon, when we heard and saw some Uzbeks dancing in an empty market place. Zhenya joined in with alacrity and of course they encouraged us. We stood watching for a while on the sidelines. Then the music got the better of us and we enjoyed the best of fun, as we twirled and swung our hips in the best Uzbek fashion, clapping our hands and getting heavily into it. It was so impromptu and enjoyable. Locally, it's considered very desirable for ladies to have these amazing heavy, black eyebrows that meet in the middle, almost looking like the wings of black flying birds. If they don't have them naturally, then they paint them in with kohl. We tried talking to them through Zhenya, but of course it was difficult to get straight answers through a man. It did appear, however, that Uzbek women are considered second-class citizens in the home and workplace – even as compared with their Kazak and Kyrgis sisters, and even though the Soviets did much to bring emancipation to women. These ladies asked many questions about us, amazed that we were travelling alone without a man between us.

On the way home Nick suddenly stopped the car, jumped out and returned with a huge bag of delicious, small, sweet raspberries, which we gorged ourselves on. When we got to the hotel, we squashed them and strained them through my T-shirt into a jug and had the most wonderful raspberry-vodkas – but wait and see my T-shirt, I doubted it would ever be the same again! Late evening, we ate at the Al Aziz Restaurant with the chaps, an excellent meal of salad, soup and shashlik. The little restaurant was beside the river and lovely and cool. Then back to the room to do battle with the bugs. On no account could we turn on the light in the middle of the night to go to the loo, the wildlife at that hour had to be seen to be believed. We complained about it to Zhenya, but nothing was done and on the morrow we would not be there anyway.

The Road to Samarkand.
Well, this was at last really and truly the 'Road to Samarkand'. We were in great form in the car listening to tapes of Buddy Holly. We sped along across flat, dusty landscape crossing and re-

crossing the Syr Daria River, consequently in and out of Kazakstan, our only visit to that country, buying yet another different type of melon in a market in Kazakstan. Then up and over the Zerafshan Mountains and into Samarkand. Hurray, the Hotel Afrosiab is clean and new. New loo, comfy beds, fridge. We were pathetically pleased to have comparative luxury – and NO BUGS now that we had, once again, become *bona-fide* tourists.

Anyway all very minor considerations when we went to have a look at the Registan Square. This is a totally mind-bending ensemble of three giant *medressas* (originally religious schools for boys, teaching the Koran and Islamic law) with almost an over-preponderance of majolica in blue, green and cream mosaics in supreme decorative designs, brilliant against the bright blue sky. This was medieval Samarkand's original bazaar and town centre. The Ulugbeg Medressa on the west side was finished in 1420, the other two, not until around 1630. I was so moved at the reality of what I'd so often seen in pictures. But obviously you cannot see the whole square in pictures and when you stand in the middle of it and slowly turn around you are just blown away by the huge, quite staggeringly beautiful place. Many of the inner rooms now serve as art and souvenir shops, which are a delight to explore. We spent some time just wandering around and gazing at the magnificence of the buildings. We wondered how on earth the American lady from the plane could bear not to get out of her air-conditioned bus – even for a few minutes – to see this majestic place.

In the evening we went for dinner with Nikolai and Zhenya; some good Tajik food made an excellent end to the day. We were becoming very good friends with Nikolai. He was quite delightful, with a lovely smile, and although he spoke virtually no English, we were able to somehow communicate with him. He was married with a little boy and was a superb driver, never giving us a moment's anxiety. He apparently drove in the entourage for Prince Charles when he visited Uzbekistan some time previously.

Zhenya, as I have said, interested me. He was very slight and young and really moved like an athlete and a dancer. When he asked if there was anything we'd like he slightly leaned forward and spread his arms wide in a graceful balletic pose. I asked him if he was married and he said no, but he was 'going to do it' that autumn. He was going to marry a Muslim Tatar and as he was Russian this would pose real problems for both his and her families.

The Tatars are a Turkic people from Russia, but descended from the Mongol Golden Horde, who began settling in Central Asia in the mid 1800s. Tall, dark and handsome, Rustam, our specialist guide for Samarkand, was also a Tatar.

It had become a little cooler, which was a relief but the days were still absolutely cloudless. Shahi-Zinda, one of the oldest places in Samarkand is a normally quiet street of tombs among which is probably that of Qusam ibn-Abbas a cousin of the prophet Muhammed who is said to have brought Islam to this area. This is a place of pilgrimage for many Muslims. The beautiful buildings were again covered in deep blue and turquoise majolica but were sadly in quite a bad state of repair. There was an air of stillness about the place, except where extensive repairs were going on. Great restoration work was being carried out with dozens of workmen clinging like flies to the exquisite blue domes. The air was full of the sound of hammers and chisels, chipping away at panels of marble. I spent long minutes watching others still, carefully painting-in small blemishes with tiny, fine brushes. There didn't seem to be any order in what they were doing but there was certainly a lot happening. In some places we had to dodge pieces of falling masonry, or duck under scaffolding. Obviously no one had ever heard of health and safety measures here; there were *no* safety precautions, you just took your chance and there would be no big insurance claims either.

Outside Samarkand at the Uluk Bek Observatory there is very little remaining of an immense astrolabe, built in the 1420s by a grandson of Tamerlane, Ulug Beg. This is on the way to Afrasiab, and the excavations of Marakanda – very early Samarkand. I didn't find this very interesting except for a room with some really striking fragments of a fresco depicting hunting, an ambassadorial procession and visits by local rulers. The colours are still good and I found this place very attractive.

The Bibi-Khanym Mosque is a gigantic, powerful building, the main gate originally was an incredible 35 meters high. It had been the grandest of Tamerlane's buildings but having crumbled away for many years, it finally collapsed in an earthquake in 1897. It was now bristling with scaffolding as it was being reconstructed but inside we got a real feel for the size of the place. It was quite amazing to look at. The glittering domes and minarets set against the deep blue sky. There was a huge market just outside the walls and we had a good look around. Again, beautifully displayed produce. Full of exotic smells and sounds. Many stalls adorned with hats and turbans and shawls of every colour and design. As we were alone, we had some really funny fractured English conversations with stall-holders whilst we bought baked apricot kernels and some spices. Then, a little apart from the general stalls, alone on the ground sat two fat ladies. We dandered over to them to see the jewellery they had on offer, smiling at them and admiring some pieces. One of the ladies asked to see a ring of Elise's and tried it on, but then wouldn't give it back! It started off more or less good-humouredly. But Elise had quite an unpleasant set-to, with a danger of it all becoming aggressive until, eventually, she was obliged to give them another ring she had, in order to retrieve the original one. In between the visits to historic relics and with no other tourists about, we normally really enjoy these meetings with local people, but on that occasion it threatened to become a rather more doubtful encounter.

The Guri Amir Mausoleum meaning Tomb of the King, houses the remains of Tamerlane, two of his sons and two grandsons, including his beloved Uleg Beg. Begun in 1403, the outer, blue fluted dome conceals the inner room, the ceiling of which is covered in the most intricate designs in 3D papier-mâché, in blue, turquoise and gold. In the middle of the room, Timur's stone is a massive block of gleaming, dark green jade.

In the evening, after a surfeit of sightseeing, we went to a very good outdoor concert in the Registan about a boy/girl folk-tale. An all singing, all dancing, rather unprofessional performance with lovely costumes and musical instruments. The evening ended up having great fun dancing all together again. I hadn't done so much dancing in years, and I had to come this far to do it.

As we were welcomed into a local family for dinner, the pungent smell of cooking mutton assailed our nostrils. It reminded me of my childhood when we often ate strong-tasting Irish mutton stew. A table groaning with food was set up in the pretty courtyard full of pots of flowers. The family were charming and very hospitable. However, as is the custom, the men of the family ate beside us while the womenfolk did all the work out back. It was all very nice until the dumplings arrived. Oh God, they are repulsive and the one Central Asian dish neither of us could stomach. They are pale, slidey gobs of dough filled with strong tasting mutton, cooked in greasy mutton fat, which clings to the roof of one's mouth for some time afterwards. We had serious trouble getting even two down and gratefully passed what remained to a very willing, Nick and Zhenya.

Tamerlane and Beautiful Bokhara.
On our way to Bukhara we went via the Zerafshan Mountains and across the Zerafshan River to visit Shakhrisabz. Although Nick was still our driver, we had another new guide: an Uzbek called Alishah. When we arrived in Shakhrisabz, he, in turn, handed us over to a local guide – a Tajik – with the prerequisite black eyebrows. She got our names immediately making a great fuss over mine being 'Diana'. Everyone recognizes the name and I get

quite a lot of reaction each time I say it, I even get called 'Lady Dee' quite often. We never cottoned on to her name. She kept calling us 'my dear ladies', which made us smile, but she was so pleasant and friendly as we exchanged facts about our families.

It would seem somewhat of an irony that President Karimov should replace Stalin as the nation's hero with another tyrant. Tamerlane wasn't even an Uzbek but a Tajik, and equestrian statues of him as a conquering hero are to be seen in many towns. Shakhrisabz was his birthplace in 1336. Between 1370 and 1405, this last great nomadic ruler succeeded in building an empire that stretched from today's Egypt to China. Although a ruthless mass murderer, Tamerlane was also a pious Muslim and a promoter of art and superb architecture such as the Registan Square.

Shakhrisabz is a fairly small town but dotted with ruins. Ak Saray Palace, Tamerlane's summer residence, no longer exists except for the gigantic 130 ft high entrance, covered in glorious blue, white and gold mosaics. If this is just the entrance, it is mind-boggling to think what the rest was like. We went to other medressas and mosques, but quite the nicest and most alive was the Friday mosque (and it happened to be Friday) and at 12 pm dozens of old men, many with long, grey beards, came shuffling in to pray and perhaps just to meet each other. They were dressed in long gowns, turbans and high leather boots. They gently greeted each other – and us – with the traditional 'Salaam Aleykhum' meaning 'Peace be with You'. They filled the mosque and then the courtyard. It was so quiet and peaceful with just the low murmuring of the men and the cooing of pigeons. Yet again, we seemed to be stepping back in time, as the three of us stood a little way apart from the mosque, at the corner of another building, trying to make ourselves invisible. These men, who could have been from another age and another world – and ourselves. What a privilege it was to be able to see a scene like this, leaving such an impression with me.

The afternoon took us across the start of the flat and featureless Kizilkum Desert. We passed men and boys on tiny donkeys often with a foal at foot. We had been having great difficulty getting petrol. It was worrying trying gasoline stations but with no success, there just wasn't any. A little cotton is grown here, but it's mainly too dry. We passed an oil well, spewing out great pennants of fire. We were still listening to tapes – 'Lady in Red' seemed to be a favourite of Nick's. Alisha was completely hopeless, we had been pleased when we got an Uzbek guide but he slept all the time in the car and contributed precisely nothing in the way of information. Maybe a manifestation of his cultural antipathy to independent women.

There seemed to be quite a bit of tourism here in Uzbekistan. Being a non-nomadic people, they are more settled and with jewels like Samarkand, Kiva and Bukhara, they have got their tourism act together much better than the other countries we had visited. Alishah did make an appearance at dinner but was still hopeless and never opened his mouth. He was no help to us at all. In fact a complete dead loss, and pushed off during our meal so we had yet another fractured conversation with Nick who, at a loss for chat, produced lots of really interesting black and white photos of himself during his naval days in Murmansk.

A local Tajik girl, Sonya, very enthusiastically took us in hand for our day's sightseeing in Bukhara. Most of the centre of the town is an architectural preserve, being more than 2,000 years old. It is the most complete example of a medieval city in Central Asia, full of former medressas, a decaying royal fortress and the remnants of a once vast market. It celebrated its 2500th birthday in 1997. Along with Samarkand and Shakrizabz, Bukhara is an UNESCO World Heritage site.

Until a century ago Bukhara was watered by a network of canals and some 200 stone pools called *hauz* where people gathered to chat, drink and wash. As the water was hardly ever changed, Bukhara was famous for plagues. The Bolsheviks

101

modernised the system and drained the pools, except those used for irrigation and as architectural monuments. The Labi Hauz is a plaza built in 1620, around one pool and is one of the most peaceful and interesting spots in town. One reclines on divans with a table between, shaded by mulberry trees as old as the pool. People and street-sellers came and went and old men drank tea or gossiped over board games. There is a fountain emerging from around the edges of the pool, which played every 15 minutes or so. Ducks, geese and storks nesting in the surrounding trees completed the picture.

The area north-west of Labi Hauz is a vast warren of market lanes and mini bazaars whose multi-domed roofs were designed to draw in cool air. Nowadays the three remaining domed bazaars are returning gradually to life, with games of *shishbesh* – like backgammon – being played, and new shops selling old and new carpets, jewellery and artefacts for tourists. Local people call the markets Sarrafon no. 1, Telpak Furushon no. 2, and Zargaron no. 3. Quite near the Zargaron bazaar is Central Asia's oldest medressa, and a model for many others – the elegant blue tiled Ulughbek medressa built in 1417.

The most famous, and I think beautiful, building in Bukhara is the Kalan minaret. When it was built by the Quarkhan ruler Arslan Khan in 1127, the minaret was probably the tallest building in Central Asia. It's an incredible piece of work, which in 900 odd years has never needed anything but cosmetic repairs. It is 47 m high with 10 m deep foundations. Included in the foundations are packed reeds in an early form of earthquake-proofing and which, indeed, have proved their worth. Genghis Khan was so amazed by the minaret, that when he was razing almost everything else to the ground, it was spared. It was also used as a watchtower, and the Emirs threw criminals off it until forbidden by the Russians. Its 14 ornamental bands of burnt brick are all different, and included the first use of glazed blue tiles that were so predominant in Central Asia under Tamerlane.

At the foot of the minaret is the 16th century congregational Kalan Mosque, big enough for 10,000 people. The roof, which looks flat actually consists of 288 small domes. Opposite is the Mir-i-Arab medressa – a working seminary from the 16th century. At the time we were visiting 250 young men mostly from Uzbekistan, had enrolled here to study Arabic, the Koran and Islamic law.

The Ark, someway out of Bukhara, is a town within a town and Bukhara's oldest structure, occupied from the 5th century right up to 1920 when it was bombed by the Red Army. Some parts of the Ark may go back two millennia, though the present crumbling walls are around 300 years old. The oldest part, the vast Reception and Coronation Court was last used for the coronation of Alim Khan in 1910. The Ark is probably best known as the prison of the Great Game participants, Colonel Stoddart and Captain Conolly. Here, the two men occupied what was known as the 'bug pit', along with rodents and various nasty insects until in June 1842, they were dragged from their dungeon and made to dig their own graves, and then beheaded!

After this exhausting but fascinating day of doing the sights, Nick, Elise and I ate in one of the medressas – Alishah disappearing off yet again – what a waste of time, and money: we have actually hardly seen him. He will get a *very* bad report. After our meal we went for tea to the Labi Hauz. It was peaceful lying on a wooden divan, with a single light bulb lighting up the green leaves above us against an indigo starry sky. Somewhere quite near, gentle music was being played on a local stringed instrument. As I listened, the musician played a series of notes eliciting from me that familiar, almost indescribable frisson of pleasure. This, was the magic of Bukhara.

The Sitori Mokhi Hosa, or Emir's summer palace is about 3 km from Bukhara. It was built for the last Emir at the turn of the century and is an amazing mix of styles. Mainly Russian outside and decorated by local artisans inside with an ornate dining room and reception hall. A 50 watt Russian generator provided the first electricity the Emir had ever seen. Next door is the harem with a, now murky, pool and a little wooden pavilion from which the Emir could watch his ladies play! There is a little museum of '*suzanas*', beautiful hand-sewn, silk or cotton needlework bedspreads made by young women as part of their dowries. It seemed so sad to have to be selling these priceless old heirlooms.

Back in Bukhara in the afternoon Elise and I went off to have another look at the covered bazaars and the warren of market lanes. The big bazaars are perfect for hanging '*suzanas*' and carpets. They are everywhere, mostly old and from both Bukhara and Turkmenistan. In some of the little shack-shops, other needlework items and jewellery abounded. Some elderly Russian memorabilia and little painted boxes were for sale, and little carved bone Uzbek people amongst other enticing objects. It was a shopper's paradise. Again here no one hassled us although everybody was very keen to sell. We walked on to the Kalan minaret area. The square is lovely, so old and atmospheric. There wasn't another soul there except two wee boys who ran away the minute they saw us, leaving us to our musings and our solitude.

Cotton-Pickin' Farewells
We invited Nick and Sonya to join us for a farewell meal in the evening. We decided we should try and go somewhere with music for dancing. We had to go to Sonya's home to collect her and her young sister, Dilya. There we met a granny, three or four other younger children and their very hesitant parents. We assured them that they would be in safe hands. When the two very pretty girls made their entrance, sadly, instead of wearing their beautiful native dress they came in what I suppose they thought very smart, but very naïve, white, children's party frocks. They had only been allowed to come if they picked a certain weight of cotton from their parents' fields beforehand. The chores had to be done before partying.

We arrived at the restaurant, complete with band and flashing lights and had quite a good meal. Elise and I both got 'lifted' for dancing by both Nick and the Uzbek owner of the restaurant. However, although being asked by several handsome young men, the two girls were far too shy and embarrassed to dance, and stuck to drinking coke. I'm perfectly certain they thought us very 'fast' with our drinking and dancing. I still wonder, did they actually enjoy themselves? They had to go off quite early by taxi but not before I had given Dilya my silk scarf, which she had been admiring and a bracelet for Sonya, which we had bought earlier. We had a great time and returned with Nikolai by taxi, to our hotel. He saw us to our room and, most surprisingly, followed us in, only to be promptly ejected by security men – it was actually quite alarming. *We* certainly had had no intention of 'any of that sort of thing'.

We were late getting to bed and had to be up again at 5.30 am, feeling absolutely exhausted, to get the flight to Tashkent. Amazingly, Nikolai, clutching a bottle of warm sweet champagne accompanied us to the airport. We had a ghastly emotional farewell from him, all of us in tears – dreadful. He had been such a great driver and indeed friend for many days and we had become very fond of him, as indeed I think he had of us. He wanted to come with us on the bus out to the plane, becoming very insistent, somewhat to our embarrassment, however, the door was firmly slammed in his face and as we drove towards the plane, he faded from view.

On arrival in Tashkent we were taken to – yes, the Shodlik Palace Hotel, the *real* Shodlik Palace Hotel, the other hick joint we stayed at before was *not* the Shodlik Palace but some other cheap joint. Silly old us. We got a rebate of $200 because of our awful hotel here the previous time. We went straight to bed for a couple of hours. Later, still feeling very tired, we took the lift down to go on a city tour. In the lift we met up with an English NGO who was in Uzbekistan as part of a conservation team which had been to the Aral Sea in order to make a report on its demise.

We sat down and listened to what he had to tell us. A sad tale indeed. Up until the early part of the 20th century the Aral Sea covered 42,000 square miles. It was rich with fish and it's seaside resorts attracted many Soviet Russian holiday makers. Then, in the 1940s, work began on irrigation canals diverting water from the huge Amu and Syr Darya Rivers to feed the thirsty cotton fields. The enrichment of the cotton fields, spelled disaster for the sea. By the 1960s the Aral Sea was losing up to 60 cubic kilometres of water a year. By the 1980s the sea was dropping nearly 10cm a month. Nobody wanted to take responsibility for the disaster. Today the Aral Sea has shrunk to about 10% of it's original size, it's fishing industry gone and the area around it becoming a new sandy salty desert.

For a city the size of Tashkent, with nearly two and a half million inhabitants, there really isn't much to see. Almost nothing remains of it's 2000 year old history, thanks to the huge earthquake in 1966 and the subsequent over enthusiasm of the Soviet architects and planners. The Navoi Opera and Ballet Theatre is almost a museum in itself, each room decorated in a different artistic regional style, executed by the best local artisans. We had hoped to go to a performance but for some undisclosed reason there wasn't one that night. The other place of some interest was the huge and dramatic Earthquake Memorial where the Soviet men and women who rebuilt Tashkent are remembered in stone. Russian newlyweds still come here to have their photos taken.

We had time before our flight to find the metro, which we had been told was well worth a look. So setting off with our trusty Lonely Planet guide we had no problem finding it, however we had no *tsum* (local currency) left and stood around feeling disappointed at not being able to go through the barrier – suddenly our dollars were useless. However the woman at the ticket-desk asked in halting English what we wanted and then let us through the barrier for nothing. We went down the escalator and lo and behold, the most wonderful station platform, all arches and a stunning painted ceiling hung with huge chandeliers while all the walls different coloured marble. Very well worth the visit.

We walked back to the hotel by way of a park with a river where some boys were playing around, jumping in and swimming and having a great time. At the airport, as usual, it was an awful performance checking in: masses of paperwork to be completed and little mini-hitlers ordering us about. We fell in with a very jolly Saga group who arrived with a lovely courier to whom we got chatting. He asked us if we ever thought we might travel with Saga, not yet of course, as you had to be over fifty. Oh yes, a very lovely courier. He was amazed that we were alone, just a group of two – it is so surprising, everyone thinks we should be with a big escorted group. But no, not for us, not yet anyway!

Riding in the Ugam-Chatkal National Park

Sher Dor Medressa, Registan – Samarkand

Friday mosque – Shakhrisabz

Lyabi Hauz and Nadir Divanbegi Khanaka – Bukhara

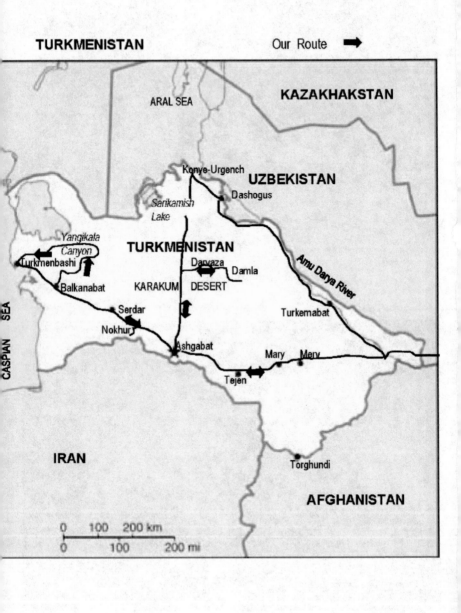

TURKMENISTAN
2009

The Akhal-Teke Horse.

... Lean in build, like the point of a lance;
Two ears sharp as bamboo spikes;
Four hooves light as though born of the wind.
Heading away across the endless spaces,
Truly, you may entrust him with your life...

Du Fu, 712 –770

Land of the Akhal-Teke.
Turkmenistan's Karakum Desert, is one of the hottest, driest, flattest parts of Central Asia and home to the fabled Akhal-Teke horse.

Although it was almost eleven years since we had first gone to Central Asia, we had loved it and the decision to go to Turkmenistan and explore a little of this country, was between us, an easy decision.

Turkmenistan lies south-west of Uzbekistan, is separated from Afghanistan and Iran by the Kopet Dag Mountains to the south, and bounded, to the west, by the Caspian Sea. 70% of the country is the Karakum Desert, a mostly barren, sometimes sandy, sometimes stony wilderness, cold in the winter and brain-boilingly hot in the summer. Its reputation as the third most authoritarian country in the world after North Korea and Burma with an equally bad record on human rights was a bit off-putting.

But, although certainly curious about it, our purpose in going there was not political and, as usual, as well as tracking down the Akhal-Teke horse, we were keen to meet and possibly stay with some of the country's semi-nomadic people.

Like all the other Central Asian countries, Turkmenistan has suffered at the hands of countless invaders, from before Alexander the Great about 334 BC, the Parthians around AD 1, The Seljuk Turks in the 1000s and Ghengis Khan in the 1220s. The modern Turkmen appeared around the late 1000s AD as nomadic horsemen, and as such had no understanding of politics or statehood. However, during this time the Central Asian countries also gained from commerce between China and India in the east and Europe to the west using the famous Silk Road – bringing a rich diversity of ideas, goods, music, literature and horses.

Terrorizing the Russians who appeared in the late 19th century with a view to 'civilizing' these disparate people, they captured and murdered thousands of soldiers, incurring the wrath of the then Tzar who finally sought retribution at the uprising at Geok Depe in 1881. The communists took Ashgabat in 1919 as an 'oblast' of the USSR until in 1924, the country became the Turkestan Autonomous Soviet Socialist Republic. Still these nomadic people rebelled against Soviet collectivisation and also the Soviet campaign against religion, and a guerrilla war raged until 1936. In 1985, Saparmurat Niyazov – Turkmenbashi – was 'elected' General Secretary of the Turkmen Communist Party and remained in power during independence in 1991. He died in 2006 to be succeeded by his health minister and dentist – and, some say his son, owing to their uncanny resemblance – Gurbanguly Berdimuhamedow.

Ashgabat.
The Hippodrome in Ashgabat is a unique experience, for racing the indigenous Akhal-Teke horse. Local young people decked out

in traditional costume parade proudly for each other, while young men perform martial arts all for our delectation. The first race was for traditionally-clad Turkmen, wearing their large woolly hats, embroidered waistcoats and black trousers tucked into long riding boots. They looked superb mounted on their prancing horses. After this marvellous display, the jockeys wear our more recognisable coloured silks. The races are over different distances, as we knew, depending upon the age of the horse. Betting is high on the agenda, legal or not with old and young alike getting wildly excited as each race concludes. The shouting and cheering was so reminiscent of racing at home or indeed anywhere in the world. 'Sport of kings', the saying goes, 'Sport of kings, commoners, townspeople and countryfolk', I would say. Watching the beautiful and proud Akhal-Teke horses was the prime reason we had come to this country.

It was cold, grey and raining in Ashgabat, not quite what we expected from a desert country. Our guide and translator, a Turkmen (I'll call him Fred), seemed grand so far. With excellent English, he also spoke fluent Russian, Turkish, Uzbek and a little Italian – not too bad. He appeared to have no criticisms of Berdimuhamedow or Niyazov and thought the former did a lot for the country. We'll see. The Hotel Nisa was unexpectedly good. We had a reasonably sized room with a little balcony facing the afternoon sun if it should deign to make an appearance. Bathroom, frig and a kettle. Our driver, Dima, was Russian. Unfortunately he didn't speak English so we could not really converse with him. We did learn that he had been the chief engineer with a construction company that went bust, so being a driver was a bit of a come-down. However, he was apparently a hunter of some repute and as such, knew quite a lot about wildlife.

What an extraordinary place Ashgabat is. Lonely Planet describes it as a cross between Pyongyang in North Korea and Las Vegas and they have just about hit the nail on the head. Now I know there was a dreadful earthquake in 1948, which decimated the city along with tens of thousands of people, and was presumably replaced with the dreaded soviet apartment blocks, but what is happening now is bizarre. Enormous, incredibly expensive, white marble edifices are springing up everywhere. Almost all of them 'ministries' of one sort or another. For instance, along with the normal sort of ministry – such as Trade or the Environment – they have a Ministry of Fabrics, a Ministry of Books (housed in an extraordinary building designed to resemble an open book!) and even a Ministry of the Horse. (I don't think it is shaped like a horse.) There are around thirteen solid golden statues of Niyazov in Ashgabat. The two which we were taken to were on the Arch of Neutrality, on top of which is a revolving golden statue always facing the sun, which still revolved even though the sun was in hiding at the time. Then there is the Earthquake Memorial. If anything, even more extreme. It features an enormous wild bull, symbolising the earthquake and balancing a globe on his horns. But Niyazov's mother, who was lost in the earthquake, is depicted tumbling into a gaping abyss, still holding up with her dying breath, a little boy – Niyazov of course, in solid gold. Such self-engrandisment is to me, incredibly unattractive, even if as Fred insisted, it was the people who wanted these statues. Apart from the usual apartment blocks, there is also a row of luxurious, Turkish-built apartments. Empty. With the Turkmen's average wage of about $50 a month, nobody can afford to live in them.

By 6.30 pm it was still lashing rain and although we had been recommended a nearby restaurant, decided we would eat in – bed! We enjoyed a refreshing glass of vodka from a bottle recommended by Dima, our driver. Then our own noodles, wine saved from the plane and short-bread, topped off with cappuccinos. It was still pouring as we put out the light. When we visited Kashgar at the western end of the Taklamakan Desert, years previously, we were told it never rains in Kashgar, well, it did. The rain of Ireland seems to follow us wherever we go, hoping to quell any signs of homesickness we might be suffering from. We had to have a dour laugh as we opened the window and heard the cars splashing along the streets below us.

Merv – Queen of the World

It had stopped raining but everywhere was damp, green and puddley as we set off east along the base of the Kopet Dag Mountains en route for Mary (pronounced Maary) and the ancient cities of Merv.

Our route took us past the ruins of Anau where we visited the old and crumbling mosque, which finally fell victim to the 1948 earthquake. Part of the main doorway remains, still with a scattering of blue and turquoise mosaics, which must originally have enriched the building. This had been and indeed still seemed to be, an important place of worship for pilgrims, particularly childless couples hoping for off-spring, there being a dozen or so of the former sitting at the feet of an old mullah while he prayed with them. He apparently sits there every day – in fact he looked as though he came from long, long ago with his long white beard and purple robes.

Further along the road we happened upon dozens of parked cars and buses and being of a curious nature Elise and I asked Dima to stop and see what was going on. Hundreds of men and women were streaming back up to the road from where we could see tents, camels, horses and a very obvious festive gathering. Fred asked what was going on and was told that it had been a demonstration of dancing, singing and riding for some visiting dignitaries. Well, damn, anyway. An hour earlier and we would have seen it all. It's a fact, isn't it, that life is all down to 'timing'. Sometimes you get it right and sometimes you bloody well miss out. We missed out. However, the people were all dressed in traditional costumes and we were able to stop some of them and take photos. The girls were truly lovely. Pretty girls in gorgeous dresses, jewellery and headwear.

We drove on along a good, wide, tarmac road, remarking at the odd-looking flat topped hills, which we could make out here and there and into the distance. On asking about them, Fred told us they were artificial hills that had been built during the use of the Silk Road to help caravans locate the direction of the route. What a brilliant idea, but such a job to hand dig these extraordinary land marks. Arriving at the ancient settlement of Abiverd the sun was by now shining in a cloudless sky full of larks singing their hearts out. This area had been renowned for its fertile land and rich crops, famous for its magnificent market and mosque. From about 652, Abiverd was governed by various notorious dynasties – Takahinds, Saffanids and Samanids. Then in the 1200s, sadly, like so many other magnificent buildings in Central Asia, the town was razed to the ground by the eldest son of Genghis Khan, the people running for their lives to the desert or the Kopet Dag mountains. It was discovered during excavations, that the city was renowned for its craftsmanship in jewellery, metalwork and pottery.

We took time to explore the crumbling, deserted town, its mud/sand houses slowly eroded from wind and rain, slipping back to join the desert from whence they came. Instead of people in the streets busying themselves with the minutiae of life, a carpet of bright red poppies trembled in the light breeze. We busied ourselves in this atmospheric place with the excitement of children, finding shards of broken pottery and glass from eight hundred years ago.

The Mausoleum of Abu Said Makneyi (Meane Baba) is situated near the small village of Tahkta, down a road to the south a few miles before Mary. It was built during the reign of the Turkmen-Seljuks in the 11th century. This mausoleum was constructed over the graves of famous followers of sufizm having a double dome that was the main characteristic at that time. The inner part of the mausoleum is wonderfully decorated with inscriptions and the doorway is laced with mosaics. Here, Fred sat us down and told us his mother was Russian Orthodox from South Ossetia and his father was a Muslim Turkmen. He had chosen, as an adult, to become a Muslim and he started to talk about Islam and its great place among the religions of the world. As an agnostic – if not an atheist – I am not good at this. I cannot bear having any religion thrust down my throat and Fred, I'm afraid, was very opinionated and rather blinkered. As far as he was concerned, there was no room for discussion. His way was the only way. We were both a bit upset at this lecture we were getting and hoped it wasn't going to spoil the rest of the trip. To Elise's horror (I had heard this theory before), he totally believed that the air crashes in 9.11 in New York were put-up jobs by the CIA to get the people of the US angry enough to support George Bush in his anti-Muslim forays in Iraq and Afghanistan. He quoted all sorts of reasons pointing to the logic of this conclusion. Although there was some substance to his reasoning, surely to God, nobody in their right minds could have concocted such an appalling scenario and consequent loss of life to their own people.

Fred was quite interesting so long as we let him talk and didn't make any interruptions with other ideas or opinions. To my total surprise he was divorced, which is rather frowned upon, with a little boy of three and now has a Russian, Christian, 'fiancé'. Fiancé means you get to sleep together on a regular basis. There is at least that much commitment, but it doesn't mean you are engaged to be married. Fred had been a junior judo champion and had travelled a lot during these championships. His prize, when he won a bout in Germany, was a car, which he then drove back to Turkmenistan. I presume this was true bill. He was obviously intelligent and well educated and would have liked to have had a better job by going into politics but, by his own admission, hadn't a hope, as he was only half Turkmen and didn't have any relations in high places. When I asked him about the Aral Sea disaster with so much water being diverted from the Amu Darya River into the Karakum canal, he said, "Turkmenistan doesn't care about the Aral Sea". What an admission.

Before arriving in Mary, we drove off-road for a break and parked beside the Karakum Canal. With the sun having just set, at this crepuscular hour the air was full of birds, while the water reflected the calm, silvery evening as we had a good long walk. The canal is the largest irrigation water supply in the world. The

117

main section from the Amu Daria to Geok Depe was started in 1954 and completed in 1967. In the 1970s and 80s it was extended to the Caspian Sea, making its total length 1,400 km/870 mi length and is navigable for 450 km/280 mi. The canal opened up huge new tracts of land to agriculture, especially cotton growing. Unfortunately, the primitive construction of the canal allows almost 50% of the water to escape en route creating lakes and ponds along the canal, and a rise in groundwater leading to soil salination problems causing the sparkling, white salt flats we had been passing all day alongside the road.

Our hotel in Mary, was perfectly acceptable. Fred took us later, to a small local restaurant where we had shashlik while being serenaded by deafening muzak for some of the locals to gyrate to. Quite surprisingly, some of the girls wore really short dresses while others wore the more elegant, accepted long dresses.

We simply could not come to terms with the Turkmen currency and spent a good lot of time counting and recounting our dosh and then bemoaning our incompetence. First of all we had to convert sterling into dollars, then into old *manats* and then into the very recent, new *manats*. As everything was priced in old *manats* we were totally confused but able, luckily, to pay for most things in dollars. Maybe, we hoped, by the end of our time here we would have sussed it out. But knowing my financial and arithmetical track record, with Elise not a whole lot better, it was doubtful.

Merv was originally known as Merv-i-shah-jahan, Merv, Queen-of-the-world – what a beautiful name. The Merv Oasis is located in what was the lush delta of the Murghab River in what is today south eastern Turkmenistan, about 200 km/124 mi north of Takhta Bazar. While it is undoubtedly geographically isolated by mountains and desert, Merv was an important node on the Silk Route, rivalling Damascus, Cairo and Baghdad as a trading centre, acting as the gateway to Persia and Rome from China and Central Asia. Merv is one of the very early centres of civilisation, a huge archaeological site covering 125 km/78 mi square, where one can see the ruins of five walled cities dating from different periods, the latest being from the 18th century. No other abandoned city shows its history as well as Merv, starting with Erk Kala, the earliest structure, dating to the early Persian period (sixth to fifth century BC). This is followed by ruins from Alexander the Great's time and later the Parthians. In 651 Merv fell to the Arabs and became the capital of Khurasan, the easternmost province of Islam.

The really unique thing about Merv is that it is a series of cities, built side by side through the ages, rather than on top of one another. I found it quite difficult to get my head around the amazing span of history that encompasses this site. The remains of the remarkable Erk Kala, as the oldest, is in some ways the most imposing site. At the foot of the huge hill, covering what used to be 30 m/98 ft high walls of the ancient city, we were suddenly accosted by a group of young women on a bus tour of the site. Tall and elegant, they made a great fuss of us, touching us and our clothes and demanding that we should be photographed together. Then while we climbed up to the top of the mound, I was aware of someone pushing me from behind and turned to discover we had been joined by a Turkmen family. They, also wanted to have their photographs taken with us. We seemed to be attracting as much interest as Merv itself – two more old ruins to fit in with our surroundings!

The site on top of the hill gave us a wonderful view of the rest of this huge area. Much of the other remains are still obvious buildings all of which we visited. Personally, I think the most dramatic is the 7th century Kyz Kala (Maiden's Castle) ruins with it's huge, extraordinary, corrugated, stockade type outer walls measuring 42 x 37 m/137 x 121 ft, pierced by narrow, wedge-shaped windows. The well preserved Mausoleum of Sultan Sanjar who died in 1157, would perhaps be considered the 'landmark' of Merv. It is said that so magnificent was its turquoise-blue dome, dominating the surrounding land, that Silk Road caravans could spot it while still a day's march away across the Karakum Desert. Although, sadly, its beautiful tiles are long since gone, the mausoleum's well-weathered dome still stands out in the desolate, ruined city of Merv, deservedly becoming a UNESCO World Heritage Site in 1999.

The exploration of Merv took us most of the day but we had time later on to visit the small museum in Mary housed in an attractive 100 year old Russian mansion. The exhibits were well displayed and we were delighted to find that they were titled in English.

We just had time to visit the town bazaar. However, being so late a lot of the fruit and veggies had gone, but we bought some delicious apples, some pistachio nuts and raisins. As ever, in these bazaars, everything was beautifully laid out in bowls and buckets. Neat pyramids of green, yellow and orange fruits, and tomatoes as round and shiny as billiard balls. As usual what was available was interesting and needless to say, everyone was interested in us. While we watched him making the dough and then slapping it onto the wall of the big round earthenware oven called a *tamdyr*, one friendly and curious baker gave us delicious, hot fresh bread to eat. These *tamdyrs* are considered to be holy so old ones are never destroyed, just left to disintegrate. We finished the day under a clear blue sky with a stroll along the banks of the Murghab River, which rises in NW Afghanistan. In Persian it is translated very appropriately, as Birds River, as we watched swallows performing aerobatics, swooping about, turning and diving, scooping up insects loitering over the water.

After only two nights in Mary, we managed as usual to make a real disaster zone of our hotel room. It somewhat resembled a cross between a stall for second hand clothes and a chemists shop with a dash of small-time groceries thrown in. I really have to tell tales on my friend here. In the evenings, Elise spent an awful lot of time pottering with her baggage while I succumbed to a second libation (I sometimes felt a bit guilty about this as we share the cost of the bottle and I drink more of it than Elise). I asked her what on earth she was doing all the time and she replied that she was organizing items of clothing, itineraries, her camera, specs, nibbles etc in the place she thought she was most likely to find them according to need, the following day. So she was always changing their places with the consequence that although in theory her plan sounded a good idea, she never knew where anything was. I asked her why she didn't always keep items in exactly the same place all the time in her rucksack. "Oh", she said, "that would make it far too easy, that's for smarty-pants like you!" Yes well, I must keep my big mouth closed and mind my own business.

Driving south, down a dry mud track, now between dun-coloured gentle foothills, we arrived at the fortress of the great ruler, Nadir Shah. It was so well camouflaged, nestling in a natural amphitheatre, built in the 18th century and surrounded by a moat. The southern wall was damaged but the other walls had remained pretty well intact. We spent some time, climbing up onto the walls and walking around, coming across a little family of three tortoises having just woken up from their winter hibernation.

Fred then asked us if we would like to visit a little village he knew of where we might get tea. Of course, we said yes and off we went to this pretty place, with a little stream running through it. It was very quiet with nobody to be seen. The village school was closed for the day – all the children having gone home. However, we found that the lady who serves tea was there with her family and we were taken by the children to a grassy bank by the little stream with a mat to sit on to await the arrival of tea. It was heavenly. Delicate, yet voluble birdsong competed with the rushing stream while overhead apple, cherry and apricot trees blossomed on laden branches. As I stood at the waters' edge, disturbed frogs leapt out of the undergrowth into the safety of the river. The children arrived with pots of tea, yogurt and sweet biscuits. Elise and Fred blew up balloons that Elise had brought for the children and off they went, unaware that they would probably burst. Suddenly, with a bang one did, eliciting loud wails, and tears of fright from the smallest child, whilst Fred blew up a replacement. I wanted to pay the lady for her trouble, but Fred said she probably wouldn't take any money. However, when I knocked at the door of the house just before we left, I was invited in. I could see just how seemingly little they had and insisted that our hostess take some money. I was glad when she appeared to be happy enough to accept the small amount I gave.

When we left the village, Fred pointed out the border post with Iran, just a hundred or so yards away. From here it was a very pretty pastoral scene with a good view of the snowy tops of the mountains.

As we approached Ashgabat, I asked Fred about the women sweeping the street. There were loads of them in the capital. What a ghastly job. These poor wretched women in their long dresses and handkerchiefs tied over their faces, just pushing around the dust on the already clean, garbage-free streets. I said what a terrible job and these ladies must be very, very poor to do such work. Fred said,

"There are no poor people in Turkmenistan, it isn't a terrible job, they like doing it. It is well paid and the women get free housing if they need it!"

I was astounded at this news. I cannot believe that anyone would actually *want* to do it. I said I supposed they had the scarves over their faces to protect them from the dust and Fred replied. "Yes, and also they don't want to be recognized". Well, that said it all really. Later, back in our posh hotel, sitting on our tiny balcony in the sun we pondered over the plight of the road sweepers. I think it would be unheard of in Ireland or England, where the streets are cleaned by big motorized brushes. But the streets in Ashkabad were clean and rubbish-free and perhaps it's better to have some sort of work rather than be jobless. I'm pretty certain there is no 'dole' in Turkmenistan.

There were several cranes and JCBs working away in the area adjacent to our hotel and Elise had been watching the goings on with avid interest. An enormous hole had appeared and we wondered what it was all about. It transpired later that the building that had been there had just recently been knocked down to make way for another ministry. In fact, just after our return home we heard that our nice Nisa Hotel had been closed, ostensibly for renovation but then we heard that it too, is for the chop to make way for – yes – yet another ministry. It's not hard to believe that the government is by far the highest employer in the country.

The Akhal-Tekes.
After the recent days of glorious sunshine, this day was dark and dusty after a lot of wind during the night. We were bound for Old Nisa and a visit to a 'racing stable' for Akhal-Tekes. First of all we stopped at Fred's house for a cup of tea. The street where he lived had a long row of garage doors interspersed with small doorways, one of which we entered. This brought us into a garage-cum-yard, which in turn contained three small rooms and a large Sky television dish. One of the rooms was Fred's kitchen, a fairly poor place but nice and warm as he leaves the gas stove lit *all the time* – as Turkenistan has so much natural gas it is free and matches are not! The other two rooms are his bedroom and a room for his father and grandfather who live with him. The remainder of the yard was an open area covered by a vine, which was just starting to come in to bud. Fred's immaculate BMW took pride of place almost filling the yard.

It was bitterly cold but dry when we arrived at Old Nisa. Again, a chorus of larks accompanied us on our exploration. This ancient metropolis, reinforced by towers that sheltered the Royal Palace, and surrounded by a thriving commercial city, was the capital of the Parthians in the 2rd century BC. One ruling dynasty replaced another until in the 13th century, the Mongol Hordes got to their dirty work again and within fifteen days had the city razed to the ground. It is really tragic that so many ancient and fascinating cities, which had already flourished for such a long time, met their untimely ends at the hands of Ghengis Khan and his cohorts. We rambled around guided by Fred telling us tales of what went on so long ago. Most of the old city has almost totally fallen down but there are remains of a circular chamber thought to have been a Zoroastrian temple. Work is going on all the time here, uncovering the past and reconstructing some of the reasonably surviving buildings.

Now it was our turn to begin visiting the horses we had come so far to see. We drove down a side street of small one-storey houses in a built up area, coming to a halt outside one of them. Isn't it interesting how you always have a scenario built up in your mind of how something should look, judged by how the same thing would look at home, so when we were told this was a small racing stable we were non-plussed. We could see no stabling, fields or gallops.

We were greeted by the owner and trainer, Balysh, wearing the Turkmen's traditional fur hat. He welcomed us, and we, him, with the normal salutation of 'Salaam aleykum' peace be with you. It's lovely, they take your hand with one hand and with the other put it on their heart. He beckoned us in towards a sort of back yard, which housed a corral containing a brood mare. It was about 10 metres wide and fenced with old bits of timber, a set of bed springs, some metal sheeting, old radiator parts and some planks, all of which were cobbled together with pieces of string. Marvellous. She certainly needed to be a quiet mare and so she seemed, as Elise went up to her and found a soft velvety muzzle, which gently nudged her, in the hope of a sugar lump or other goodies, which we had forgotten to buy.

Five other horses were housed in – to us – the most rudimentary stabling up the yard. They were brought out one by one to a patch of sand on the side of the road. If you know horses at all, you will know how they prepare for a roll, almost crawling along with bent knees for a pace or two before succumbing to the luxury of a really good roll. Each one in turn did exactly the same thing. Unusually, to us, they didn't shake themselves afterwards but kept the sand on their coats. They were trotted round for us to inspect and a prize-winning, black stallion was made to rear at the command, which was very dramatic. The horses all seemed to have a lovely temperament. They stood about 15 to 15.2 hands high and moved with the grace of a dancer, as an old horsey friend of mine used to say, 'Just hitting the ground here and there'. They have a naturally proud, high head carriage and quite long sharp-tipped ears. None of the stallions are gelded and all are raced from two years upwards. The 2-year-olds race over 1,400 m/4,593 ft and 3-year-olds and upwards, over 4,000 m/12,000 yd. So quite long distances compared with the UK and Ireland. No whips are allowed on the youngsters, which is wonderful. There is no handicapping system so obviously a good horse will win everything. They had no bedding and were fed mainly on alfalfa, carrots, corn and sugar. All were getting fit for racing which was due to start any day.

This was a real family affair. Balysh, the trainer, his brother Maksat, the jockey, and countless other male relatives all helping with the exercising and stable care. The family had been racing Akhal-Teke's for seven generations. They have quite obviously very little money and both men had to go to do other work in order to afford keeping and racing their horses. Their silks were homemade but at least Maksat wore a sort of very flimsy crash helmet when he went racing. The only female we saw, as usual, was the pretty daughter of about fourteen.

We were invited in to the house for tea, which of course we accepted with alacrity, and were shown into a room, bare except for Turkmen rugs on the floor. Cushions and mats were produced for us to sit on – not a chair in sight. In fact the sole piece of furniture in the room was an enormous television set with accompanying video and CD players. A program was on about the

Akhal-Teke. We talked horses and racing and were invited to watch the gallops early the following morning.

On a whim, on our way to visit the mosque with the biggest dome in Central Asia, I asked Fred if we could go to church the following day, as it would be a Sunday. He said of course that would be fine for us to go to the Russian Orthodox church. I said we would like to go to an Episcopal church. But no, there is no Episcopal church in Ashgabat, but then I don't suppose there would be too many Episcopalians in Turkmenistan, although I do know that even in Belfast there is an Islamic centre and mosque. This new and huge mosque that we were visiting, is called the Turkmanbashi Ruhy Mosque. It is most dramatic from the outside with four minarets soaring above the golden dome, each one 91 m/298 ft tall, representing the year 1991 of Turkmenistan's independence. Inside it has a rather beautiful ceiling as well as the most stunning and unbelievably extravagant, hand-woven, eight pointed carpet. The mosque is built about 11 miles out of Ashgabat in Gypjak, Niyazov's (Turkmenbashi's) childhood home. It is reputed to hold an amazing 10,000 souls.

We had a very late lunch of barbecued lamb and shashlik in a busy outdoor café surrounded by flowering trees and shrubs. With music and lots of young people it was much more fun – and far cheaper – than the dreary indoor cafés we had previously frequented. On walking back to the hotel we passed a large archway into what looked to us like a park. The large lettering on the arch was naturally enough in Turkmen, but looked something like 'Market Bejasus Salad Haberdashery'. We were laughing at our fractured attempt at translation and Elise was just taking a photo, when I noticed three official-looking men standing watching us, nudging each other and, I thought, looking a bit threatening. It was just then that I saw, in smaller print something about 'ministry' and you are forbidden to take photos of ministries. I quickly told Elise to stop filming as we were being watched. We assumed a casual air, smiled at the men and walked on. Whew! Now maybe my imagination was running riot, and it probably was, but we decided not to take any more photos of anything that could conceivably be a ministry. We walked on by way of a bookshop, which had been closed earlier. There were some beautiful books in English, on the Akhal-Teke horse, which we drooled over, but they were very expensive and terribly heavy, so bought, instead, some rather nice, postcard size, pictures of the horses with names, breeding and descriptions on the back.

We had been talking at some length with Fred about music when he told us he had gone to music school and when asked by the head master what instrument he played when he first went there, had said the clarinet. He had in fact, never played the clarinet but simply loved the sound of it and although it took second place to his love of judo, he evidently became proficient at playing the instrument and developed a real love of classical and modern music. A man of many parts I thought. We said we went to orchestral concerts at home and would be very interested in going to hear some Turkmen music in Ashgabat if it were at all possible. No sooner said than done. Fred arranged to pick us up at the hotel and true to his word, there he was at the appropriate hour dressed in an immaculate light coloured suit with 'the fiancée' and driving the BMW. We had cleaned up as much as possible with our very limited wardrobe, but I had applied some make-up with mascara and eye shadow, which Fred immediately noticed and complimented me on. So my effort wasn't all in vain. We thoroughly enjoyed an evening in the Magtymguly Theatre which is huge and ornate and filled with an enthusiastic crowd. The program was a mixture of old and modern Turkmen music and dance. The girls looked gorgeous in their colourful dresses, and even if the singing was not completely to our taste, the dancing was graceful and very pretty. There were some comedians who as well as speaking, mimed so well that even Elise and I saw how funny they were. Everybody else must have thought they were hilarious, so much so that they almost brought the house down with whistling and cheering.

Before setting off for home with his girlfriend, Fred left us off at one of his recommended eateries where we waited simply ages for a meal but which, when it came was very good. Everywhere we have eaten in the evenings the food was much better than expected. However, the restaurants were awful. Soulless, empty, filled by loud music, and with a sort of cheap Chinese-type décor but always very, very friendly staff who did their best to please us. Nevertheless, we asked Fred, to aim us at more local-friendly eating places.

On our way back to the hotel, we passed a family of mother, father and small child. As we approached, the child looked up at Elise, and without more ado, and to all our surprises, took her hand. Elise and the dad proceeded to give the child swings between them to everybody's delight and amusement. Of course we had no words in common, but shared laughter and a bit of fun with the little boy was all it took to give us so much pleasure.

We had to be up by 5 am on the day we went to watch the training gallops. We met up with the family at the stables where five horses were being prepared for exercise. They set off in advance of us then we followed Balysh in his car. We drove about three kilometres to an oval gallop, set up a slight hill with a backdrop of river and mountains. The limpid, very early morning light, lent an almost ethereal quality to the scene. 'Hail to Thee, Blythe Spirits.' I silently greeted the host of larks singing above us. To begin with the horses just walked round the track, their warm, exhaled breath puffed into little clouds in the cold air. Then as they went faster, they went round the track singly. The black stallion went first, a couple of rounds quite slowly, then as he increased his speed, he fought to be allowed to go faster. With his high head carriage, his ears were almost in the jockey's face. I don't think he could have been stopped at this point even if Maksat had wanted to. Increasing speed round the top bend he came towards us flat out, tail streaming, jockey and horse as one Maksat lying low on his horses withers, whose unshod hooves thundered on the sandy ground and passing us in a flash. It was one of those moments in life when something quite normal becomes a very special moment, exciting, dramatic and very moving.

The other horses followed suit with one young two-year-old being ridden bare-back, becoming very excited and starting to play up. A couple of two-year-olds went round together at a gentle canter without being allowed to feel the excitement of what it is like to gallop. They were not at all sure what they were supposed to be doing looking around with curiosity as they were ridden quietly round the track.

We were invited back again for tea and noticed in front of the house, on the road-side, a little fire. Fred saw me looking at it and said that it was burning rubbish. Good idea I thought but then when he showed us how they had taken a lead from the mains gas pipe and lit it to burn the rubbish, we found it highly amusing. Free gas, so why not?

Meak (pronounced Me-ak), the pretty daughter, showed me photos in one of the rooms, of her great grandfather riding a horse. This family is so involved with their horses, they are a way of life and their whole raison d'etre. She disappeared off to another outside room where some women were boiling water and finding some sweets for us. Meak, because of her youth, was allowed to join Elise, me and the men for tea but when it came to taking a family photograph she reneged – as is patently obvious from her scowl in the resulting photo. She watched our every move with huge curiosity, smiling to herself as she watched us ungracefully lowering ourselves into a sort of sitting position to take tea. She was however, delightfully hospitable, thanking me graciously when I gave her a pretty silk scarf I had brought for her.

Sunday is the day for both horse racing at the Hippodrome and the Tolkuchka Bazaar. This being so, we rose early again (is this a holiday or what?) A long queue into the parking lot kept us a bit late and when we did eventually get parked, we were told how to spot our Land Rover and not to get lost. We fought our way through the packed crowds at the bazaar. *Tolkuchka* is aptly named, in Russian meaning 'little push' – it's more like 'big push' and if that doesn't work, try shove. It was all great fun though. Word had it that this bazaar rivaled even the Sunday market at Kashgar, but not to me anyway. Kashgar was in a league of its own. Even so, this market was enormous, covering 50 ha of land. Carpets were perhaps the most evocative merchandise on sale. They were quite stunning. When we were in Bukhara some years previously we thought *it* was the home of Central Asian carpets, but there we were told that they were almost all made in Turkmenistan. So here we were, surrounded by the rich, red carpets woven almost exclusively by women, they are used as wall-hangings in the nomad yurts as well as floor coverings. It was tempting to price them and get stuck-in to a bit of haggling, but neither of us really wanted, or indeed needed a rug, so we pushed on to the hat stalls. Wonderful hats made from the wool of the Karakul sheep; black, curly Persian lamb hats, fox hats and little skull caps. We tried some on and good for Elise, she bought a very jaunty fox hat. Scarves and textiles, embroidered slippers, Russian memorabilia, coral and turquoise jewellery. One entire lane of gold jewellery and an enormous area given over to cheap Chinese clothing, herbs, fruit and nuts. Sacks of spices and bunches of dried flowers.

Now then, I have to say a word or two about the Evil Eye. This is the belief that some people can bestow a curse on victims by the malevolent gaze of the 'magical' eye. The most common form attributes the cause to envy, with the envious person casting the Evil Eye, most probably unintentionally. Belief in the Evil Eye, amazingly, is almost world-wide especially in the Americas, Middle East, East and West Africa, South Asia, Central Asia, and Europe, particularly in the Celtic regions.

Somewhat surprisingly, we learned that belief in the evil eye is found in Islamic doctrine, based on some of the verses of the

Koran, 'And from the evil of the envier when he envies,' and the statement of Prophet Muhammad, 'The influence of an evil eye is a fact'. Aside from these Islamic beliefs, a number of unsubstantiated beliefs about the evil eye are found in folk religion, typically revolving around the use of amulets or talismans as a means of protection. It is to these talismans that I now refer. Near the area of the spice vendors, we noticed these bunches of dried flowers called *yuzaerlik*, which along with rams' horns and dried peppers, are hung outside houses to protect the inhabitants from the Evil Eye. Sometimes the *yuzaerlik* is burned and the smoke used to disinfect the building and drive out evil spirits.

Beyond these exciting stalls and outside this main market, there was a huge area full of second-hand parked cars all for sale. Literally hundreds of them, and more like a graveyard for ancient Ladas than a saleyard... How any could be taken for a trial run was a mystery as there was absolutely no room to swing a cat, let alone a car. Then on to the livestock market. Camels being herded by every means, even craning them ignominiously, bellowing, urinating and teeth bared, up into carts. All types and breeds of sheep, some of them we had seen before, the 'fat-tailed' sheep with their huge, rather gross bums. Goats, cattle, chickens, ducks, even a not-so-proud peacock. People having picnics, haggling over prices, leading home newly acquired animals. Noisy and exhausting but certainly all the fun of the fair.

Taxis in Ashgabat
Getting a taxi in Ashgabat is a novel experience. We had decided to go to a very flashy-looking restaurant some distance from our hotel, so Fred said to take a taxi. He told us to wave one down, anywhere, and wrote the name of the restaurant on a piece of paper. OK, fine. We smartened ourselves up for this foray into the fleshpots of Ashgabat, left the key at reception and asked whether we would be able to get a taxi near the hotel.

"Oh yes, of course, its easy," we were told by the pretty receptionist. So, off we set. The road the hotel was on was very quiet so we decided to go to the main road up the street. This was a mad thoroughfare, but nothing daunted we crossed the road and waited for a taxi. We waited and waited but none were forthcoming.

"How on earth do we know when it is a taxi?" I asked Elise.

"I haven't a clue," was the unhelpful answer.

"Well, what do we do now?"

"Go back to the hotel and ask them how to do it."

So saying, we started back across the busy road; there are traffic-lights, but they are just that – not for pedestrians. So you get into the middle of the road and then wait and make a dash for the other side as soon as there is a break in the traffic. We were helpless with hysterical laughter. I had to sit on some scaffolding I was laughing so much.

"And now we are going to have to admit that we don't know how to get a taxi, two elderly and well-travelled ladies who can get themselves to all arts and parts of the world and can't get a taxi!"

It seemed daft and absolutely pathetic. Nevertheless, back we went to reception to a most surprised young receptionist.

"We don't know how to do it," admitted Elise.

"Don't know how to do what?" asked the girl.

"We don't know how to find a taxi, what do they look like?" asked Elise while I sniggered behind her.

"It's easy," said the girl. "You just wave one down, it will stop and you get in."

"Fine" we said, "would you ask your porter to do it for us, please?" By this time we were both feeling embarrassed, old and stupid.

The porter came with us back down the steps, stood for a couple of minutes on the kerb until the first car came along, then he just waved it down. It stopped and waited for instructions. Easy-peasy. *Any* car will do we discovered. "You mean this is legal and OK?" Well not exactly legal but everybody does it we learned. In we hopped, the porter telling the driver our destination.

The Minara Restaurant was on the top floor of an enormous circular shopping mall in Independence Park. Inside, the shops were quite small and poor, nothing like the big flashy merchandising emporiums of the West. The outside was totally covered with waterfalls floodlit at night. It's quite extraordinarily over the top – the building and the restaurant. The views from our table were great both inside and out. The menu was varied, one item, Squirrel Salad, we decided to forego. Sadly and as usual, there were only two other tables in use.

Back again outside we sauntered down the park to the main road discussing whether we would be brave enough to flag down a car. In point of fact, there was no option as we hadn't a clue how to get back to the hotel – and it would have been a long walk at that. Arriving at the kerb, I stuck out my hand and before you could say Jack Robinson a car pulled up. This time with two youngish fellows – one each, we murmured to each other. They knew the hotel and off we sped. I have to admit we were both a fraction anxious. One chap we could possibly overpower, but two? We sat holding hands giggling nervously, saying nothing but separately our imaginations working overtime. Let's face it, who would want us? Far, far too old for the white slave trade! It seemed ages longer than the ride to the restaurant, before we arrived happily, safe and sound back at our hotel. I suppose the flip side to having a bad human rights record is that people behave well and there is very little crime. Interesting.

One Dubious Jockey.
We had not originally been intending visiting the Arkabask Stud. But just before leaving home we had been advised that the couple who owned the stud we were supposed to visit, had been thrown into jail for non-payment of taxes. Wow, how about that for draconian measures? The Arkabask Stud is about 50l km/31 mi

south-west of Ashgabat. This visit had been set up for us from the UK, but still we wondered just what it would be like after the surprise of the last racing stable. However, this was in a much bigger way of going. We were met by the owner, Ashir, who, with his suede jacket and tweed cap could easily have passed for an Irish trainer. We were taken into the stables, a long row of loose boxes all occupied by a range of Akhal-Tekes. Each one was described to us, its breeding and racing results. Swallows whizzed around the roof, chittering as they went. It was great to see so many swallows. There must have been dozens of them, so at least they seem to be breeding well in Turkmenistan. However, this was not what we were there for as I concentrated on listening to the history of the horses. As is my wont, when indoors with horses, I got a fierce attack of hay-fever and started sneezing my head off. I departed for the outdoors and waited for the others who emerged in a few minutes. We made our way into a sand school where one by one the horses were brought for our inspection lead by a young groom in baggy trousers tucked into long boots and a shaggy wool hat. The first horse was the epitome of the Akhal-Teke, a beautiful golden dun colour with a very distinctive metallic sheen. There was enough room here for them to really show off their paces as they were trotted and then cantered up and down. Then, again each one had a good roll.

The Akhal-Teke horses of this region are reputed to 'sweat blood'. It was thought for many years that this was due to their thin skin and when heavily exercised blood burst through their skins. It has been discovered however that the bleeding is due to a parasite that is picked up in drinking water. At a certain point in the lifecycle of the parasite, it breaks through the skin causing the bleeding. This bleeding is known to occur in other animals such as donkeys and cattle, but not people. We asked about the horses sweating blood but Ashir hotly denied the theory that it was caused by a parasite. Well, I suppose he would wouldn't he, it's more glamorous to sweat blood because they have such thin skins, than to be afflicted by a parasite.

We chatted horses and racing until a bay mare was brought out for us to try riding. Elise was really up for it but I could feel my courage dissipating as the morning drew on. However, the mare was fine, quiet and willing and we both passed the riding test. Apparently some French men had come to the stud to go riding having said they could ride but before they even left the farm, three of them had fallen off. Consequently, Ashir vets all prospective jockeys before he lets them loose on the range. Elise was allocated the bay mare as being the more confident rider and I was given a black stallion who was a little smaller, but quite feisty. These Akhal-Teke horses move so well they are a pleasure to ride, and behave well while on the move, but ask them to stand still and they become fidgety and restless, pulling at the bit, their heads going straight up into the air. I thought I would be OK if we could just get going, but when a mare whinnied near-by, my stallion became so excited that I could just imagine the pair of us disappearing up the yard to go and attend to her needs. I nervously demanded to get off pronto before any extra-curricular activities could take place. Of course Elise was bent double laughing at my discomfiture.

We waited around while someone went off on a motor bike to collect a second saddle from a neighbour. I don't think they thought we would actually go riding having seen what age we were. Ha – they ain't seen nothin' yet! I was then allocated a little hairy mare straight out of the field and once we got saddled up, off we went, a stable lad on the black stallion in the lead followed by Elise and me. We had the most lovely afternoon in the sunshine, riding along beside a little stream through huge wheat fields sprinkled with scarlet poppies and yellow and white daisies. All the horses walked out well without having to kick them along. After a while our path began to climb and became rougher and quite stony. If we had had more comfortable saddles we could have gone on forever, as it was, both of us had to keep taking our feet out of the stirrups and stretching our legs. As we headed for home the stallion quickened his pace, then Elise broke into a canter. Finally, as tail-end-Charlie I too forgot my former qualms and in order to keep up with the others, gave my little mare her head, thoroughly enjoying the gentle canter back towards the stables. But oh, how I wished we were 40 years younger.

On the way back to Ashgabat, we visited Geok Depe. This site includes the remains of the fortress of Geok Depe and modern Sapamurat Hajji Mosque. The 19th century fortress stands where a particularly bloody battle took place – the Turkmen's last stand against the Russians in 1881 – when the Russian Empire attempted to conquer the Turkmen. During Soviet times the area was a collective farm, but today the large Sapamuret Hajji Mosque, a modern building with brilliant blue domes, commemorates the 15,000 fallen Turkmen during their last battle for freedom. The mosque was erected after the President's pilgrimage or 'Hajj' to Mecca and was completed in 1995.

After the long, very successful and tiring day we persuaded Dima to stop to buy some juice. He took us to a huge square with an enormous supermarket on one side and a row of 'dukas', or little shops opposite. We have yet to see any sort of smart shop or department store. Coincidently, this sort of little shop is also called a 'duka' in Kenya. It must be something to do with Swahili being an Arab language. I always felt that Fred, being a teetotal Muslim, was faintly disapproving of our predilection for vodka, but that Dima was quite amused at our reliance on him to 'see us right' in buying what we wanted. We added some fruit and nuts and enjoyed our usual preprandial refreshments on our little balcony, until it became too chilly to stay outside. We found the weather much more changeable than we had expected. Probably the end of April or early May would have been warmer without being too hot. We decided to eat in the Italian restaurant on the ground floor of the hotel as it had a good reputation. The minute we were seated we were immediately looked after by the Italian gentleman who had the franchise for the restaurant. He was full of chat, pleased to meet Europeans and interested that we had come to Turkmenistan as curious travellers. Most of the other residents in the hotel were on business. He had come to Ashgabat in 1991 at the time of independence and had stayed on, intrigued by how things would work out. Business had been good for him, but he was now fed up with government policies and restrictions and wanted to go home to Italy.

Westwards to Nokhur.
Nokhur is an unusual region with a culture of its own, in the western Kopet Dag Mountains. Our route there was punctuated by a visit to watch the Arkabask gallops and to Kov Ata underground lake.

The previous day we had understood from Fred that we would be watching a race between the horses from a grandstand. It didn't quite come up to our expectations. We followed Ashir's car into a complex of sand dunes used by the locals as a dumping ground. Oh dear, Fred was dismayed that we should have seen such a place. I should have thought it was terribly dangerous for both horses' feet and cars' tyres. What with broken bottles, tin cans, scrap metal and sundry other items, any of it could have caused damage. The grandstand was the top of a sand hill and the race was between only two horses. A certain amount of 'lost in translation' I thought. Again, the fine, early morning was filled with birdsong as we waited and waited for the horses to appear. Then we saw through the binoculars that a flock of sheep were being herded across the track by a very slow shepherd. Then two camels wandered into view, shambling down the track. Eventually the camels deigned to turn off to the right of the track and disappeared from our view. Our excitement grew as we watched the now clear 'race course'. Into view came the two horses, barely cantering. Ashir shouted and gesticulated to them to get a move on until as they grew level with us, they started to actually gallop. What an anti-climax. This so-called professional stud couldn't hold a candle to the fun we had had with the small-time trainer, Balysh.

Kov Ata is quite a tourist spot for the locals. You enter a huge cave, dimly lit and buzzing with hundreds of birds – pigeons mostly, swallows and swifts. A long set of steps takes you 65 m/200 ft underground to a sulphur pool, renowned for its curative properties and naturally heated to around 36°C. It so happened that when we were there, Elise and I were totally alone. Even then, there was no way in the world that we would have donned our cozzies and launched ourselves into the dark, tenebrous depths. As we emerged back into the sunlight, a busload of ladies with two men, all chattering excitedly, pondered the advisability of taking the plunge.

Visually, Nokhur is quite unlike any other site found in Turkmenistan. We took a left turn up a side road, the very flat desert plain seeming to go straight uphill into the mountains. Rich in history, nature and tribal custom, Nokhur is set 1,100 m/3,000 ft above the Karakum Desert in the cool mountain valleys of southwestern Turkmenistan. The Nokhur people have maintained a society based upon ancestral rights, and tribal custom. Constructing their homes from the stones found around the area, the Nokhur people have decorated these simple homes with hand carved wooden columns unique to their clans. Varied images in the stunning silk, woven by local Nokhur women, indicate their particular tribe, making Nokhur silk renowned throughout the country. The Nokhur felt rugs are also thought to be exclusive to this region. They differ from customary Turkmen felts with their original Zoroastrian designs and ornaments, symbolizing the worship of fire and the cult of fertility.

We arrived about noon. Large by local standards, Enebai and Gaib's house was our destination for the night. We climbed up the steep path and into the roasting hot, totally unfurnished front room. We were shown our room, about 3 m/9 ft square, and more or less as expected having seen Balysh's house, totally bereft of any furniture except for red patterned rugs over the floor. Hm, interesting. We looked at each other and were wondering what to make of it, when we were brought tea which was put on a tablecloth on the floor. Then some rugs and cushions appeared so we lounged on the rugs and had green tea and sweets.

It was strange because during our previous travels in Central Asia, we had always had beds. And even our homestays in Kamchatka had had beds and chairs, so I suppose we were a tiny bit surprised when we didn't have these comforts in Turkmenistan. Oh well – it was all part of life's rich tapestry so we just had to get on with it. We unpacked our sleeping bags and thin little foam mattresses and went to meet the family. They came and went into the front room, so over-heated by a wood-burning stove. Enebai, our hostess was a tall, imposing looking woman dressed in a long purple dress with a patterned shawl over her shoulders and a tight-fitting head-scarf, quite different from those in Ashgabat. Her dark-eyed, dark-browed, strong face lit up with a smile as she took us to see the new bathroom, which was approached from outdoors, under the house but complete with a shower. Then she took us to the loo – or long-drop. We followed her along the road and then down some very rough steps and a little rocky path. Amazingly, although it was a good 100 m/328 ft from the house, it was lit by electricity and had twin holes. Aha, never pee alone – take a friend along. So we did. Without going into too much detail, my partner managed to splash my trouser-leg bottom. "You owe me," I said, outraged. "Big time." Needless to say, the apologetic response was lost in an expected guffaw of helpless laughter. We decided that we wouldn't have anything to drink too late as it certainly wasn't for the faint hearted to make a night-time trip to that loo.

None of us were hungry as we had had barbequed lamb already at Kov Ata and so we went exploring Nokhur. The cemetery is a really interesting place to visit. Each grave was adorned by at least one pair of mountain goats' huge, curved horns. This as I described earlier, is believed to ward off evil spirits. It was quite a large cemetery to wander round until Fred and Dima appeared to show us the way up a path to Qyz Bibi, a spiritualist, Muslim shrine. Here, folk from all over the country come on pilgrimage. Further on and up a very rough path of 269 steps, is the mausoleum of Parau Bibi. According to local lore, Parau Bibi was a virtuous young woman who, when she heard that an enemy siege was imminent, prayed that the mountain would swallow her up rather than be ravished by the barbarian tribes. Obligingly, just in the nick of time the mountain heard her plea and swallowed her up. Later, the local people honoured her by creating a fertility shrine on the spot.

The road up into the high pastures and (we were told) a spectacular waterfall, passes two huge and ancient Plane trees, hollow with age. Highly revered, they spread their massive branches at will knocking blocks off elderly buildings, their dark shadows stunting the growth of other plants below struggling for a glimpse of sunshine. The road twists upwards, a tough walk indeed eventually coming to an impressive, rocky, tree-lined gorge through which for millions of years, a deep river had flowed. As we stood on the plateau above the gorge, we could see across it, a steep cliff where the river fell hundreds of feet. The only thing was, the river was just a trickle and from where we were, there appeared to be no waterfall at all.

However, nothing daunted, we continued on down a steep track and round the end of the gorge to where the reasonably sized river should have been. It was so tiny that we could cross it on stepping stones. What a shame. What water that did fall over the edge would surely have disappeared completely before reaching the ground so far below. The clear, sparkling little stream was very pretty bouncing cheerfully down the mountain. We picked our way up-stream and thence to a small farm situated in a little valley surrounded by flowering apricot trees. Fred spoke to the farmer who said that there had been very little rain so far that spring. Indeed there had been much less snow than usual that winter, which, with the snow-melt at that time of year, normally would have produced lots of water for the river. Quite a serious situation at a time of year when water should have been so plentiful.

We met up again with Dima and the 'landy' and proceeded on upwards for half an hour or so. Then off we went again – all four of us – on foot, up and up, guided by Dima who knew of a cave to explore. Eventually we came to the snow line, melting now in the hot sun and exposing lots of wild flowers. We had to slip and slide down a steep slope, round a bluff, very rough under-foot and slippery with patches of snow. We arrived, in deep shadow, at the mouth of the cave, our entry into it blocked by a drift of snow. Dima, doing his version of Sir Walter Raleigh instead of spreading his cloak for us, kicked and bashed at the snow until it was low enough for us to scramble over and enter the cave. Giving us his hand in turn, we slithered down the rocky floor into the dark depths. We wished we had known to bring our torches but they were of course back in the house.

From the cave up to the top of the mountain at 1,981 m/6,500 ft wasn't too difficult, mostly rolling upland dotted with shepherds cabins. We were able to avoid most of the patches of snow and arrived – very pleased with ourselves – at a small cairn with views all around. Although it was a cloudless blue sky and we should have been able to see further, it was quite hazy down into the Nokhur valley.

Back at the home-stay, we were asked if we liked *plov*, a rice, carrot and meat dish and as we like it very much, were glad to be able to be genuinely pleased to accept it for dinner. Our meal was laid out on the floor of another room on a big tablecloth surrounded by rugs and cushions. Our men were already seated cross-legged waiting for us as we plonked ourselves down with about as much dignity as a couple of elephants. I had watched Enebai earlier, sitting down. With years of practice, she put one foot behind the other and just sank gracefully into a cross-legged position, her long dress curving neatly under her bottom and round her ankles. If the food had been on a table it would have been groaning under the weight of all the goodies laid before us.

Meat balls, *plov*, bread, sweets, yoghurt and a sweet drink made from rose-hips. It was a delicious meal but enough for an army.

After dinner we went to see the family silk loom in a separate house. We learned that in this part of the world, marriages are arranged but with agreement from both parties. One of the daughters-in-law had been married only recently. So with respect for her in-laws, she would cover her mouth with a silk scarf when being addressed and only talked to us or Enebai through another member of the family. She came with us to meet yet another daughter-in-law who was busy at the loom. They brought forth for our delectation, a selection of beautiful silk scarves in a variety of colours and clan designs.

We decided not to waste the lovely calm evening and set off for a twilight stroll down through the village and back up to the house via numerous back gardens. We emulated a group of tethered goats, as we passed them scrambling up a narrow bramble strewn path, arriving breathless, conveniently back at the two-stander loo. Careful not to have anything at all to drink, we sorted out our bed-time paraphernalia until we had each made as comfortable a sleeping place as possible.

We discovered that Enabai had been honoured in Soviet times by being made a Hero Mother. She was indeed a hero mother – I would have said also an Earth Mother – having produced five sons and three daughters and now the proud granny of 18 grandchildren. This honour had brought her a good pension and huge social standing in the village. However, after independence the pension stopped along with that of thousands of other pensioners. The great Niyazov had discovered that he had vastly overspent his budget by building all those grand 'palaces' so in his wisdom reimbursed himself by siphoning off the old peoples' livelihood. Enebai, living up to her heroic reputation soon used her initiative by opening up her house to visitors and starting the family silk-weaving business and now had made a good life again for herself and her family.

Another lovely morning saw two lady travellers walking downhill from Nokhur towards the main Ashgabat/Balkanabat road. We had enjoyed a breakfast of sweet, warm camel milk, fresh bread with honey, yoghurt, fruit and green tea. The boys were to follow and pick us up after taking the car to be washed. It was a lovely walk even though it was on the road. Through high cliffs beside the tumbling river our walk was made more interesting by the amount of people who stopped to offer us lifts which is a very friendly, prevalent habit hereabouts. I don't suppose it's often that the locals find two elderly western ladies making their way, unaccompanied, down the road.

When in due course we were back again in the car, we drove along the main road with flat sandy wastes to either side. Suddenly Dima stopped the car for us to have a look at a big flock of handsome, long-legged birds feeding at a green, obviously damp spot. He couldn't remember the name of the birds, which he said were migrating from Iran to Northern Kazakhstan to breed, but said they certainly were not storks. With my on-coming cataracts, even with the binos, it was quite difficult to identify them but I think they were perhaps, cranes.

As we arrived at a meagre-looking little building at the side of the road, we discovered it was a café, which served strong black coffee. Wonderful. We also bought some chocolate from the two women who lived there with a small toddler. There seemed to be a tiny living space behind a net curtain, separated off from the café. Although situated on the main road, but miles from anywhere else and in the middle of the desert, they cannot exactly have done a roaring trade.

As we drove on with the road deteriorating, the Kopet Dag mountains eventually ran out on our left-hand-side. We were approaching the Balkan Massif, otherwise we were on totally flat, sandy desert. An hour or so later we arrived in Balkanabat. Having been directed to the Ruslan Restaurant we took no time finding it. Yet again, having waited around three quarters of an hour, we were served an excellent meal with beers. Our dinner that evening was also excellent with for once quite a few other diners seated at neighbouring tables.

An alternative to Camping at Yangykala Canyon.

For the forthcoming trip to the Yangykala Canyon, we had a back-up vehicle – in case of accidents – driven by a young, very shy, Uzbek called Maxim. However, with Fred guiding the way we were only about 10 km/6 mi out of Balkanabat when we took a wrong turn up a side road which ended at a quarry! Not a good idea. Dima was annoyed as we had to turn and retrace our steps all the way back to Balkanabat. Fred was gracious enough to take the blame and eventually led us up a different road to the north-west out of the town, through a poverty-stricken looking village and into the desert again, camels grazing on what they could find amongst the sparse tufts of grass.

By lunchtime it was dull and cold, the desert now consisting of rolling hills, enlivened by the golden heads of the *Shomuch* plant. One of the Angelica family which, when growing as densely as in these parts, lends a warm, golden tone to the otherwise dun coloured desert. The local people cut the plant at its base, boil the stems then strip and press them using the resultant liquor for digestive purposes.

We stopped for a picnic lunch in good old Irish drizzle. Miserable and chilly, I remember thinking, 'Are we right in the head getting ourselves first of all lost, then cold and wet, miles from habitation?' However, back in the car and before long, the road – or track – started climbing steadily towards a plateau surrounded by cliffs. The Yangykala Canyon.

This has to be one of the most dramatic and breathtaking places I have ever seen (so far, I have not been to America's Grand Canyon). Part of the allure is of course the silence and solitary isolation in the desert. The Cliffs of the Canyon are between 60-100 m/196-328 ft high and stretch over more than 25 km/15 mi all the way to the Karabogas Gulf on the Caspian Sea. The immense, soft landscape of layers of pink and white rock, change from yellow-orange to rust-red in the rain. This huge area is totally empty save for hundreds of swifts whizzing about. On top of the plateau, coming to terms with these surreal remains of an ancient, evaporated ocean even such an unbeliever as I could well believe its grooves and folds had been formed by the hand of God.

Thanks to my friend and Professor-Emeritus of Geology at Trinity College, Dublin, I was able to discover the scientific background to the Canyon. It would appear that the whole area has all the hallmarks of a post-glacial flood spillway. When the Quaternary Ice Age was at its peak, and the great Eurasian ice sheet was covering northern Eurasia, its weight pressed the earth's crust down and the downward warp caused the region south of it to bulge up. Much of the total ice-cap melting occurred in two brief, rapid spurts separated by about a thousand years during which the climate returned to Ice Age conditions.

It would appear that around 12,500 BC, the enormous flood of meltwater from the melting of the great Eurasian ice sheet fed dozens of great lakes that no longer exist. These filled the sag in the crust caused by the weight of the ice as the ice retreated. The lakes swelled and flowed southward to the Aral, Caspian and Black Seas each spilling into the other. The breaches created incredibly fast erosive floods filled with glacial debris, which carved deep, vertical-sided canyons.

The Yangykala Canyon may well have been one of these, probably created when the hugely enlarged and deepened Aral Sea overflowed and broke through the bulged crust to its south. Subsequently with the total melting of the ice sheet and the end of the flow of meltwater, the climate of the whole region warmed up. Many of the lakes dried out and disappeared and the present arid aspect of the landscape was established.

We spent ages walking to ever more spectacular viewpoints, waiting for the sun to make its tentative appearance from splashes of blue sky in between the clouds, enhancing the furrows and colours of the cliffs below us. We must have taken dozens of pictures. The plateau was a cobweb of tracks, making it really difficult to find the right ones and we kept having to back-track to find the right direction encouraging me to say to Fred. "It's really hard to find your way here, it must take three or four times exploring to learn about the area and find out where to go."

"For a woman, yes, but I knew my way after only one time," came the reply.

I couldn't believe my ears. We had already, early on, taken a wrong route, and here we were constantly having to retrace our steps and he had the brass neck to say he knew where to go.

"Ah yes," I said, "but of course you are very special."

My repost was taken with complete equilibrium but I could see Elise's shoulders shaking with silent laughter. But he was really incredible. So chauvinistic and self-important at times, yet kind and thoughtful at others.

We had originally allowed ourselves to be talked into camping here for the night but Fred and Dima both thought it was too cold and windy. So we were given the option of spending the night in a tent in the cold and wind or staying at a sort of hermitage or small place of pilgrimage. The thought of high winds in this already wind-swept, barren spot wasn't too encouraging. I could just imagine us, tents and all being swept off the edge of the cliff. So we plumped for the hermitage about two hours drive away. We had been warned that the elderly man and his wife who lived at this place and were custodians of the little mausoleum, were very religious and didn't allow alcohol. As a consequence of this, we poured our evening refreshments there and then and toasted each other against a backdrop of the canyon, under a blue sky and low, golden sunshine.

Gyzli Ata Mausoleum is the resting place of a respected Sufi teacher of the early 12th century. The teacher had a large following until his untimely demise at the hands of – yes – the

Mongol invaders. His mausoleum and the grave of his wife is now a popular place of pilgrimage and includes a small graveyard. It is diligently cared for by the elderly Karim and his wife, Oguolgarek, or Olya as she is known. It was dark by the time we arrived and the three men were greeted by the elderly, bewhiskered Karim and whisked away to talk men-talk. Elise and I were ushered into a room by Olya – her small frame enveloped in layers of long garments and sporting yet another different type of headscarf. It was not tight round her face but almost as though it had a hidden peak inside, keeping the scarf away from her forehead but wrapped, warmly, round her neck and chin.

It was obvious to us, from the evidence of a bowl of food and two spoons, that two people had been eating on the floor. With gentle courtesy, our new hostess showed us in and beckoned us to sit down. She removed one of the spoons and produced two more, which she gave to us, then gestured for us to tuck in. My heart fell. Oh God, what will it be like? I'm not going to get away with this one I thought... We had no Fred to translate or make excuses so we just had to get on with it. It was in fact, delicious. A sort of Turkmen/Irish stew with very tender meat. Naturally, we had not a word in common, so Elise gesticulated the type of animal in the stew. Two fingers on top of her head and a jumping motion meant rabbit. No, Olga shook her head. I did big horns and big leaps for a gazelle. Olga rocked her hand back and forth, so it was something like a gazelle. We did baa-ing for a sheep. No, not a sheep. We were all laughing by now and when Fred reappeared, we discovered that we had been eating baby goat – kid. And very good it was too.

With a total dearth of conversation, Elise and I produced our family photographs. This always works well, as it is obvious that they are of our children and grandchildren. Photos of our homes are difficult as they look way too posh. But we have photos of the countryside, old Irish churches and castles. Of course we also have photos of Strangford Lough, which always elicits much interest, the people of Central Asia living such a great distance from the sea. So with these pictures, we are able to have remarkable 'conversations'. When Fred came back into the room, he said, "I knew it, women always manage to make themselves understood to each other." Ah ha. So we do have some assets after all.

While Elise was rummaging around in her bags, I asked Olya to show me where the toilet was, thinking it would be just round the corner. She guided me round the end of the house and up the path of a huge full moon towards four little huts. We passed one little hut on the way, which I gesticulated to but she shook her head and giggled softly. Only for family, or perhaps the men, I presumed. It was about 100 yards to the row of long-drops, each a few feet apart. She waited while I made use of one and then accompanied me back to the house.

When Fred reappeared, Elise asked him if we could see where we were going to sleep. "Here," he said.

"Oh, but this is Olya's room," said Elise.

"Yes, I know, but you will sleep here tonight, the other rooms are too cold."

"But what about Olya, where will she sleep?"

"Here," said Fred.

"Ah, right… OK… you mean all together?" faltered Elise.

"Yes, of course, is that not alright?"

"Oh, yes of course," we chorused together.

And so it was to be. First thing, we placed our bedding with our heads against the wall, but Olya changed them to the middle of the floor. Our heads must face east, she insisted. I showed Elise to the kazies on a night when the moon shone so brilliantly across the desert, from a cold, clear sky. A night made for romance I thought longingly, not a lot of it around here this evening.

We can rough it pretty well, but really hate going to bed without cleaning our teeth. So we mimed teeth cleaning and were rewarded by Olya jumping up and returning with a basin of warm water from the ewers in the fire outside and two mugs of cold water. They always kept two or three elegantly shaped big fire-blackened ewers, always in the fire with boiling water at the ready then it was poured into other, cleaner ewers for use. Ablutions accomplished, we made our way to our beds on the floor. Olya had taken off her outside coat, outer trousers and over-dress and scarf and was sitting on her bed waiting and watching our every movement. We were too embarrassed or respectful to watch her. "Are you going to get undressed?" I asked Elise.

"Not much," she replied.

We take so long getting ready for bed. Between us we have to attend to dentures, hearing aid, asthma inhaler, contact lenses, spectacles, ear plugs at the ready for insertion, pills to take for one thing or another, face and hand cream to apply etc. etc. I got the giggles as we fiddled about, thinking how quickly Olya had become ready. She just hopped into bed without any pre-nocturnal preparations in comparison to the performance we had to go through. What an uncluttered life. Finally, leaving a torch at the ready in case of emergencies, we were ready for the arms of morpheus as we lay, like three sardines in a tin, only inches apart, our heads in the middle of the room facing east.

As I lay there before sleep overtook me, I wondered how often I had thought of values the world over. From Olya's life to ours was such a far cry. At Gyzli Ata we were seriously out of our comfort zone. I wondered how she would cope with our home surroundings and life. Perhaps rather better than we did in her home, certainly with a lot more dignity. We are inclined to giggle – not at the other people, rather at our own inadequacies and discomfiture when faced with a life-style so different from that we knew. Squat toilets – totally appalling to many folk from the UK – no chairs, sleeping on the floor, boiling water on an outdoor wood fire, the woman of the house doing *all* the chores while the men sit, putting the world to rights, *beside* the fire. It is tempting to have the inclination of being sorry for people who appear to be so poor and have very little in the way of possessions, but in fact their lives are probably much less cluttered than ours. Our western world has become so money orientated and materialistic that we seem to spend a lot of time trying to deal with it all. I often find myself wondering what quirk of fate intervened that I should have been born in relative prosperity. In a country where it is commonplace to turn on a switch for light and a tap for, at the very least cold water. But at the end of the day, are we any more content than the family in Nokhur or our hosts in Gyzli Ata?

We slept remarkably well. I could just make out Olya moving around in the early morning, stoking up the outside fire and preparing a simple breakfast of bread, margarine, green tea and yoghurt. It was bitterly cold as we made our grateful farewells beside the fire. Yet again, the huge kindness of complete strangers. We certainly paid them something, but nevertheless we arrived unannounced and they were obviously not prepared for an influx of five. A chill wind was blowing and the sun only just up as we made our way to the Land Rover and motored off again into the desert.

It was no time before we encountered an elderly Toyota car, well and truly stuck in the deep, soft sand. A young man and four women – all scantily clad – were standing around looking helpless. We were about to pass them when Elise and I both asked "Are we not going to help them?"

"Of course," said Fred, "but we didn't know if it would be OK with you."

My God, you'd have to be some sort of a devil if you couldn't stop and help – and us in a Land Rover. Dima, Fred and Max got out to survey the situation. The occupants of the Toyota looked frozen to death. The women were wearing very light, long dresses, without a coat between them, so we beckoned the girls into the Land Rover to keep warm. An older lady was shivering so violently it made the entire car tremble. We had to take several efforts at pulling the Toyota out, finally succeeding by dragging it backwards, out onto the vague tracks of the path. I think they were pilgrims on their way to Gyzli Ata, so I sincerely hope they arrived all right.

The Caspian Sea Enquiry.
We arrived at Turkmenbashi, the large port on the Caspian Sea in time for lunch at the smart Hotel Turkmenbashi. We sat – yet again – in solitary splendour with a view of the Caspian Sea. This is not exactly the most glamorous of cities, but it is reputed to be quite cosmopolitan, probably the reflection of its multi-cultural population from countries around the Caspian Sea. We could have made our journey even more exciting if we had caught the ferry to Baku in Azerbaijan – but then, we'd already been there! The city used to be called Krasnovodsk when the first settlement was established in 1717 by Russian troops under the command of Prince Alexander Bekovich. However, they didn't stay long and it was over 150 years before the Russians returned. The town grew in importance with the building of the Trans-Caspian railway in 1880. The difficult feat of engineering, mostly in terribly hot conditions, took the railway across hundreds of miles of desert, eventually reaching Bukhara and Samarkhand by 1888. During WW2 it was used to transport thousands of Japanese prisoners of war who were put to work constructing roads and houses. There is still a handful of nice old buildings dating back to the early 1900s.

As it was, I had a project from a friend at home who was trying to get evidence that the, now rare, Caspian Seal was being caught in poached sturgeon nets. I had arranged to go and visit the director of the Hazar National Reserve Park. In my ignorance, I had thought that a 'park' would be somewhere outdoors, possibly on the coast with a sea-water pool. I should know by now never assume anything. We were taken to a little museum with a dusty collection of stuffed seabirds and ducks. We initially met a very friendly woman, who wanted to charge us a lot for a guided tour. A guided tour of what? Twenty or thirty stuffed birds, when I wanted to find out about seals. So we asked about the seals and were lucky enough to be able to meet a Mr Berdy Berdyev, the deputy director of the 'park'.

Upstairs in his office, he told us quite a bit about the program. A Memo of Understanding between the Institute of Integrative and Comparative Biology of the University of Leeds, and the Kazar State Reserve of the Ministry of Nature Protection of the Darwin Initiative Project, titled the 'Quantification and Illimination of Threats to the Caspian Seal'. Whew. He said that an invasive comb jelly known as *Mnemiopsis,* which arrived in the bilge water of ships using the Volga-Don system some years previously is out-competing the native plankton. This, in turn, is causing a decline in the kilka, which is the basis of the Caspian Seal's diet and is a major factor in the problems facing the species. I think, perhaps, he had a selective memory about the other major factors including over-hunting of seals for fur. When I made the observation that the seals might be being caught in sturgeon nets used for poaching, he totally dismissed the suggestion with an abrupt "Niet." Ah well, I didn't really expect to get an affirmative answer, but it was a most interesting interview.

I was both surprised and pleased that we had been able to meet Mr Berdyev, and reiterated my appreciation of the interview to Fred saying how very kind of him to see us at such short notice. His unbelievable reply was, "Well, it wasn't very kind of you to keep talking to each other when he was talking." We were both absolutely speechless. The only reason we talked was Elise recounting to me what Fred was translating from Berdy so that I could get it written down. I said this to Fred, but of course it fell on stony ground. In any case, it was incredibly rude of him to criticise clients – who, of course, are always right!

The train from Turkmenbashi to Ashgabat pulled out of the station on the dot of 3.30 pm. Fred had tried to convince us that we should return to the capital in the car with Dima and himself. But we rather like trains, and although it would take us until the following morning going at a leisurely pace and Dima would be back in the middle of the night, we stuck to our guns and insisted on our plan to go by rail. We discovered that, in fact, Fred hates the train as he doesn't sleep well. "Why are you coming with us in that case?" We asked him. "We will be perfectly OK without you." Having been unaccompanied on the Trans-Siberian and the slow train to China, from Vladivostok to Harbin, we could certainly manage the one night in Turkmenistan.

"You are not permitted to go alone," we were told.

"Heavens," we replied, "We are hardly going to jump train in the middle of the desert."

"It is not legal," Fred replied.

Well that was that. We found our compartment for two, with Fred ensconced next door on his own. The attendants were all very helpful, polite and kind, telling Fred if there was anything at all that we should want, just to let him know. We chuntered slowly out of the station, with the Caspian Sea on our right-hand-side. We passed docks, oil refineries, the ferry terminal and warehouses before approaching the beach, which we ran alongside for half an hour or so. On the left-hand-side we passed grim looking apartment blocks, each small concrete balcony harbouring a sky television dish. A little further on, as the landscape rose into a cliff face, stood the little pale blue Russian Orthodox church, a reminder of Turkmenbashi's early Russian past.

Very quickly, the buildings ended and we entered a desert landscape again. We were very lucky to spy some wild horses standing knee-deep in a rare meadow of wild flowers, and always, here and there, camels roamed. As there was no restaurant car on the train, we had brought our usual stand-by rations: Pot Noodle, wheaten biscuits, bananas, yoghurt, lemon juice and finished off with packet cappuccinos. I don't really know what the huge attraction is for trains. I suppose there is something old fashioned and romantic about them. Travelling at a sedate pace and when you are ready, making your bed and snuggling up for the night. Of course, these trains stop pretty often during the night and the screeching brakes and consequent juddering before grinding to a halt wakes one up. After Balkanabat, the train was full and Fred complained about having to put up with his co-travellers, so the lucky boy was given a compartment to himself. I presumed he'd had to pay the difference but he confessed that he knew the attendant who let him off the extra payment.

Still in darkness, we arrived in Ashgabat early the following morning. As we walked away from the station, we turned back to view the pretty building, floodlit against the black sky. The station and station clock are the only remaining old Russian buildings that survived the earthquake of 1948.

Darvaza, Damla and the Desert.
The flock of sheep came into view at precisely the right moment. In the grey evening, it seemed as though the thirsty desert had drained all light and colour from the day. Elise and I had climbed a hill above the fire crater to get a better view before night ascended. Then, from our right-hand-side, the sheep, herded by a boy on a motor bike, crossed below us in front of the crater, putting the extraordinary spectacle of the fire crater into perspective.

Earlier that day we had set off north from Ashgabat on the road that eventually ends up in the north of Turkmenistan at the old city of Konye Urgench and thus into Uzbekistan. We went through the village of Jerbent some 160 km/99 mi from the capital. As it was spring, here and there the desert sported a green 'beard' of young grass. But gradually, due to over-grazing and the cutting down of Saxaul trees for fuel, the desert is encroaching more and more and Jerbent is gradually being consumed into the sandy wastes.

Our first stop was at a water and gas crater. One could smell the gas as soon as we got out of the car. It appeared that the water was boiling, but it was gas escaping from the earth under the water, surfacing in a mass of bubbles. Further on, there was another gas crater, this time it was a witches' cauldron of bubbling mud, reminiscent of the mud pots we saw in Kamchatka. They of course were boiling hot, these are cold, as again it is escaping gas. The village of Darvaza used to be situated near here. However, according to the following report from Turkmenistan, at the end of June – beginning of July 2004...

President Niyazor issued a decree, following which the residents of the village of Darvaza situated 200 km/124 mi to the north of Ashgabat, were forcefully displaced to other villages, and the village destroyed. The main source of income of the residents of Darvaza (with a population of 3000), was sheep and camel breeding, as well as their private roadside cafeterias.

At the beginning of June, when flying over Darvaza to Dashoguz [in his jet], President Niyazor commented on the unattractive appearance of residential houses and roadside buildings and ordered the village to be destroyed. About three weeks later, some 200 soldiers and policemen arrived in Darvaza and announced the forced displacement of its residents. According to a report, a driver, working on the Ashgabat-Dashoguz motorway, had said:

"We were given one hour to pack our belongings. Soldiers pulled up with trucks heading for Ashgabat and loaded them with household wares and other belongings. Nobody even tried to protest, knowing that it was useless."

The report continued:

The displaced persons were given the following choices for their new places of residence along the motorway: the village of Bokurdak (330 km/108 mi north of Ashgabat), the village of Jerbent and some areas nearer the capital. The displaced persons were not provided with any housing. Authorities promised to allot melleks (plots of land) to them, but they have not kept their promise so far. Many of the displaced persons live in yurtas (nomad's tents) at present. Displacement completed, the Darvaza village was demolished by bulldozers. Obviously, the authorities were worried about the possibility of former residents returning to their native place. According to one witness, "even the recently built mosque was destroyed." Only a police checkpoint on the border of two velayats is now left of what used to be the village of Darvaza.

We didn't know this commentary above at the time. Fred had told us that, right enough, the village had been demolished, but his reason was that someone must have done something really bad to warrant such a punishment. Whatever the truth, it was a shockingly radical move to destroy a village and its inhabitants. Later, in the car, I asked Fred if a Turkmen reporter wanted to write in a newspaper about this sort of occurrence, would he be free to do so. It was lucky I was looking at him as I waited for his response. He looked straight ahead, unable to meet my eye and just shook his head.

Nowadays, Darvaza's claim to fame are the gas craters, man made in the 1970s by Soviet-era gas exploration. The third of these, the fire crater is something else altogether; a 50 metre-plus hole in the ground – on fire. And has been for the past 40 years. One theory goes that while drilling, geologists accidentally found an underground cavern filled with natural gas. The ground beneath the drilling rig collapsed, leaving a large hole with a diameter of about 50-100 m/164-328 ft. To avoid poisonous gas discharge, it was decided to burn the gas. Not the best idea in the world I should have thought. Another theory is that two differing gases escaping together could have caused instantaneous combustion, but then why the crater? However, the veracity of neither of the stories can be substantiated and although frustrating, what the truth was, really did not matter. It was just a most amazing sight as we walked round the blazing inferno.

We made camp in the shelter of a small hill to the south of the crater, pitching a tiny tent for us two ladies, while the men made a fire and Dima prepared a delicious supper of potatoes and chicken kebabs. Elise and I climbed the hill opposite for the view of the crater when the sheep entered the picture. Back down at the camp, as usual, we lolled around on the ground beside the fire, until I had the brilliant solution of sitting on my big bag and leaning against the side of the landrover. Such comfort. Unfortunately, Fred had, for reasons best known to him, laid the 'table' some distance away from the warmth of the fire. So we had to persuade him to move the cloth over to where we were sitting, both of us now comfortable and toasting beside the fire. We each had a shot of Elise's Irish whiskey as it seemed the more appropriate and warming libation, while we watched Dima playing cook for the evening.

Gradually, as it became darker, the drama of the crater unfolded, the smoke and fumes lit up from the fire beneath, visible for many miles around. 'The mouth of hell' is what the locals call the fire crater. Curiosity as ever, got the better of us and we wandered over to it again. In the dark it was appalling. The smell of gas was strong and the heat intensifies as you approach the edge. Oddly, the floor of the crater is not fire-blackened, just the walls are black. There are hundreds of separate fires fuelled by separate jets of gas all roaring away together. I was terrified that the adventurous Elise would go too near the rim of the crater, the thought of it making me paranoid with fear as I kept shouting to her not to go so close. Back at the camp, Fred was telling us about one time when he saw a hawk diving for a little bird above the crater. As we fetched our binoculars and watched, lo and behold, in the sky above the crater, you could see throngs of little birds brightly illuminated from below. As we watched, a hawk eerily came into view above the birds. For moments it hovered, then stooped towards its prey. More hawks arrived with repeat perfomances. Through the binoculars every feather of their outstretched wings was brightly etched against the black sky. It was a quite extraordinary experience to watch this drama being played out. There must have been some reason – a fluke of nature that brought the small birds to congregate above the fire only to meet their untimely deaths at the beak and claw of the predating hawks.

During the night the wind pounded the little tent, buffeting the thin material against our heads. The tent was really far too tiny for two, especially as Elise is so tall, she would have been more comfortable lying diagonally across it. Eventually, it awoke me enough to get out of my bag for a little dander across the desert. The boys were asleep around the fire, tucked up in blankets. The wind dropped a little as the cold grey light of dawn crept imperceptibly across the desert brushing our little tent with dewy fingers. I crawled back into the tent, defending myself from the flapping with my pillow and snuggled back down into the still warm cocoon of my sleeping bag and drifted back to sleep. I wonder how many times we have sworn never to go camping, ever, ever, ever again.

Our 90 km/55.9 mi desert drive to the village of Damla the following morning was all that a drive in the desert should be. That is, pretty damn exciting as we frequently lost our way. Even though we were using GPS we somehow found ourselves much too far north. Damla is not far from being almost due east of Darvaza, so we had to re-route to go in an more south-easterly direction. Then we became stuck in soft sand several times and had to dig ourselves out. From time to time on the vague track we were following, we passed what looked like diamonds sparkling in the sand beside us, but sadly it was only salt crystals glittering in the sun. Any habitations we passed were small and terribly poor. The people were helpful with directions and would send us on our way again. One homestead boasted a handsome hunting dog, very similar to the lean and athletic Afghan hound. What wildlife we saw – lizards, ground squirrels and a desert fox – somehow eaked out an existence from their arid surroundings, while always above and around us, larks sang and swallows chittered. I am always interested in the flora of whatever country I am in, and was constantly getting Dima to stop the car so that we could examine some of the exotic and plentiful wild desert flowers.

The day wore on until after a picnic lunch we topped the rise of a sand dune, and there below us was our destination – a biblical scene – the village of Damla. The small square houses, flat-roofed, were exactly the colour of the desert. One white-washed house at the far end of the village was pointed out to us as the headman's house and our refuge for the night. We could also distinguish some of the inhabitants playing, we thought, on a see-saw. As we stood there taking in our surroundings, we watched as some small boys, having obviously suddenly spied us, came pelting up the hill to where we were watching. Laughing and chattering they looked at Elise and me with ill-concealed curiosity. Before too long, little girls arrived to join in the welcome party and to our amazement, when we produced cameras, clamoured to have their photographs taken. Such a delightful welcome. Virtually all the children were dark with dark brown eyes, but a couple of little boys – twins I think – were to our surprise, distinctly fair-haired. Throw-backs, to Alexander the Great (a very long shot) we were told! They were all poorly dressed, some bare foot, some in flip-flops, in which to our amusement, they could run backwards – downhill. As soon as we could prize the children away from our cameras, we all hurtled down the hill into the village and to the headman's house.

Down in the village we were welcomed by an overall scent of wood-burning fires. We were shown into the yurt where we were to sleep that night and met Hajy, the headman and owner of around a substantial 500 sheep and 200 goats. He sat with his wife and family, gently nursing his recently born grandson. Two pretty daughters in their late teens or early twenties, hid their faces from us as is the custom, while another quiet little grandchild sat close by, watching us with mild curiosity. The yurt was about 4 m/13 ft across with a live fire in the middle, the smoke *mostly* going up through the hole in the roof. I noticed everyone had fire-blackened hands as we were given cups of green tea.

We decided to explore the tiny village and see what went on with the locals. However, we had only gone a short distance when 20 or so children clamoured around us, wanting to talk, play and have their photos taken. We played all sorts of games with them without having to try and talk at all. Very popular was grandmothers' footsteps where we had to catch any body we saw moving, eliciting gales of laughter from everybody. There was one particularly cheeky wee girl with hair tied up in bunches who started making faces at me – and then stuck out her tongue. I feigned absolute horror. She giggled and did it again so I did it back and she was horrified and then delighted. This started a game of who could make the worst face. Many years ago when my children were little, one day, to keep them quiet while driving the car, I pretended to be a wicked witch, hunching my shoulders over the steering wheel, pulling a terrible face and uttering a blood-curdling cackling laugh. To this day I still do it for my grand-children, eliciting the same reception of shock and then laughter. So I did it for the children of Damla, only waggling my hands at the side of my face. It must have been a bit of a shock, as one child ran off screaming in terror while the others, after a moment of total amazement, reacted as my grandchildren by trying to out-do my efforts. I really felt I had taught these lovely children something rather horrible – but great fun.

During this pantomime, the children took us to visit their families in different homes. At one house we visited, a tiny new baby was being swung furiously in its cradle by an over-enthusiastic sister, while all the other kids whispered "Shussssh," to us. Another visit was to a bewhiskered village elder carrying his young grandchild. At several houses we saw the adults using a see-saw. Not totally for fun, but for pressing the juice from the boiled *shomuch* – the plants we had originally seen in the desert. The stalks had been softened by boiling, then stripped of their outer tough skin and pressed to obtain the juice. So the see-saw was a fun way of doing it. Another system we noticed was in the form of a lorry jacked up and then lowered onto a bag of the mix making a very practical, heavy and ingenious weight for pressing.

Exhausted with all the chatter and laughter, we made to return to the yurt, on the way spying a camel being milked in a small corral. We watched as an older lady tied a rope round the camel's hind leg, pulling with all her, albeit meagre weight, while the baby camel drank in turn with a younger lady doing the milking. We supposed the leg-pulling was to stop the camel kicking the lady doing the milking.

Back at the yurt, we, our boys and Hajy, were plied with another delicious meal of *plov* – the ladies, naturally, back in the kitchen. We were offered vodka by Hajy who poured himself a glass-full. Dima also accepted as did I – it would have been churlish to refuse. Hajy made a toast, as is customary, toasting Elise and me and wishing us a good and peaceful night and favourable onward journey. Then Dima made a toast to us both, saying he hoped that when he would be our age he would be as "enthusiastic, physically fit and as much fun" as we were. What a lovely thing to say. Both Elise and I were really touched by his words. I replied for us both, thanking everyone for their kindness and hospitality and for giving us such a wonderful time.

Our night was spent alone in the yurt. The fire had been made up for us last thing before everybody went to bed. Having a fire in the bedroom reminded us both of childhood at home, before the days of central heating. When one was sick and in bed, our mothers allowing us the unqualified treat of having a fire in the bedroom. First thing in the morning – before daylight – Hajy came in stealthily carrying a lighted ember, encouraging the dead sticks into life once more.

After early breakfast, we asked if we could see the school. The day before, some of the children had shouted "skola, skola". However, being the evening the school was closed, but keen to see it now in the morning, we stopped to find out what was going on. The little school had several teachers, one teaching Russian. They were impressed that we wanted to bother visiting them and were as interested in where we came from as much as we were interested in their teaching. Term time was more or less over for the summer, as of course the families, being semi-nomadic, take their children with them when they go to the summer pastures, so there were only about six pupils remaining. It's a quandary as to whether the children should remain for schooling, or go with the family to learn about their traditional way of life. Hajy said he didn't think the village would exist in another 30 years. How very sad, but I suppose inevitable. How lucky for us to have had the experience of the village and the privilege of being welcomed into another traditional home.

Our return journey across the desert was only slightly less exciting than the previous day in that we only lost our way once. However, the Mitsubishi, which wasn't anything like as versatile as our Land Rover, kept getting stuck in the sand and had to be dug out. Eventually Fred decided to drive and poor Max had to eat humble pie in the passenger seat. While this was going on, Elise decided she would like to have a go at driving the 'landy', so with her inevitable confidence and *joie de vivre*, she took over the wheel for a highly exciting experience through and over the dunes. Even with Fred driving, the Mitsubishi ground to a halt twice, up to its axles in soft sand. Not a very reliable desert car. Unkindly, I gloated, as Fred now had to eat humble pie. He was so supremely self-confident, almost to the point of arrogance, that I couldn't help having a little smirk to myself.

Every so often, Dima would point out a wide, shallow, dried up river bed, which we crossed and re-crossed. The Uzboy River, he haltingly explained, had been a tributary of the Amu Darya or Oxus. The river had flowed through part of the Karakum Desert until the 18th century when it abruptly dried up, destroying in the process, the Turkmen civilization which had thrived along its banks from at least the fifth century BC. When the water which had fed the Uzboy abruptly stopped flowing, the tribes which had inhabited the river's banks were dispersed, the survivors becoming nomadic desert dwellers. Now, as a dry river channel it is a center for archaeological excavations.

Our track again was like a roller-coaster, causing both Elise and me to feel quite queasy. We would stop from time to time for a leg stretch and some water or bread and cheese, dancing, incongruously in the desert with Fred and Dima, to 'Lady in Red', with happy memories of Uzbekistan.

Back with the delights of our hotel, we decided that evening to treat ourselves again, to dinner in the Italian restaurant, as we had discovered I could pay with my Visa card – the only place you could use a credit card. Having started to tuck into our wine and dinner, Elise suddenly jumped up from the table and rushed off in desperation, sadly to loose the lot! She had been feeling a trifle unwell all day but rotten for her and not the most auspicious way to end such a magnificent adventure.

Istanbul and Home.
High drama in Istanbul. After a horrendous flight where we flew through black clouds with thunder and lightning buffeting the plane. The conditions effectively transformed our means of flight into something resembling a ping-pong ball, bouncing about all over the sky. We both sat strapped in, grim-faced and teeth clenched. The next drama was in the airport where we discovered we had to wait in a long queue for an hour and a half for boarding passes for the onward flight to London. It was all so inefficient, and so, also, thought several other travellers. The man in front of us was getting more and more angry, until at last when he arrived at the check-in desk he totally 'lost it'. Fuming – almost with sparks flying – saying how inefficient Turkish Airlines was – the inefficiency, of course, had been in Ashgabat. Elise joined in agreeing with him and vociferously egging him on. At the same time at the next desk, a large Arab gentleman in a flying *djlabaya*, was also having a fierce altercation. The decibels rose by the second with everybody joining in and both of us encouraging our man as he demanded to see a supervisor. The atmosphere became so volatile that I started to get the giggles. It actually was not funny. Of course we should have been issued with onward boarding passes from Ashgabat, as we had been on our outward journey. Anyway, it was all great fun and put in a lot of time, as we retired from the fray to await our onward flight and home.

Pure-bred Akhalteke horse

Two girls in traditional costume

Yangi Kala canyon

Darvaza Fire Crater

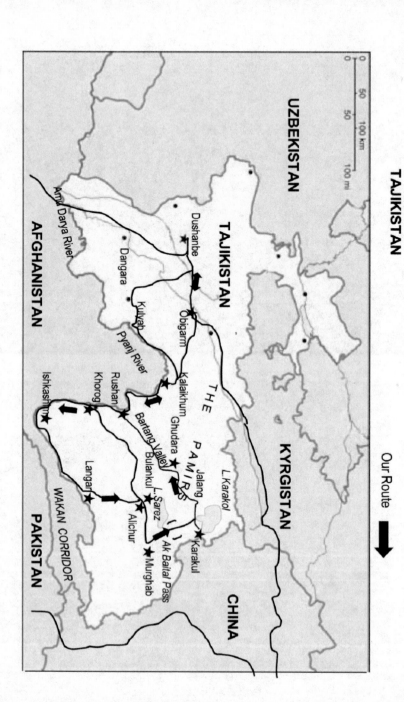

TAJIKISTAN
2009

Through the black Tartar tents he pass'd, which stood
Clustering like beehives on the low flat strand
Of Oxus, where the summer floods o'erflow
When the sun melts the snows in high Pamere;

Sohrab and Rustam
Matthew Arnold, 1822 – 1888

Tajikistan. The central country in the convoluted frontiers that form Central Asia. Guardian territoryof the High Pamirs – the *Bam-i-Dunya* or Roof of the World. Life spring of the mighty Oxus or Amu Darya River, which flows west across Turkmenistan and Uzbekistan into what's left of the Aral Sea. Separated from northern Afghanistan by a 2000 kilometre border along the Panj River. It is also, geologically, probably one of the most unstable countries in the world.

Like the other countries of Central Asia, Tajikistan is an ex-satellite of the former USSR and like the others, independent since 1991. Elise and I had originally intended coming to Tajikistan in 1998 entering from China, but the country which had had a bitter civil war from 1992 to 1997 and was closed to visitors. Now safe and at peace and with a relatively stable government, we decided that it was time to venture into this little-known country.

We spent a long time organizing this trip. Most operators wanted to send us via Uzbekistan and/or Osh in Kyrgistan, but as we had already been to these areas it seemed unnecessary to return. I was determined to try and do a circular route as it really goes against the grain to have to retrace ones steps. I decided on a round trip of the High Pamirs, returning to Dushanbe via the Bartang Valley and suggested it to the operators I had contacted. Not one of them were happy to send us through the Bartang Valley. Too dangerous they said. Rock falls, flooded rivers, nowhere to stay, all sorts of difficulties. However, eventually we found a Tajik operator called Somon Travel based in London, who were happy to fall in with my requirements. Were we daft or what? Neither the Lonely Planet nor Odyssey's new guide to Tajikistan gave any description of the upper Bartang Valley – no wonder – the authors had never been there. (We didn't know this until our return.) We gave it due consideration and went ahead and made our booking. We were the first clients Somon had had, and no one from the firm had been to the upper Bartang either! Ignorance, however, is really no excuse.

Dushanbe, Kala-i-Khum and Afghanistan.
We left Kala-i-khum and Mirov's hospitality driving alongside the river and the Afghan border. Silt-grey and white-foamed, the Panj River came tumbling towards us; a swirl of glittering water in the early morning sunlight. We turned an abrupt corner with a little stream flowing across the road having brought with it a small fall of stones. Our eyes were glued to the country across the Panj, to be rewarded with views of men on donkeys going about their business and a small village having some sort of a holiday, with women and children playing on the sandy beach. The scene of children running races and jumping down some small dunes struck us both as being far from any war. Then – absolute nothingness. A donkey track scratched a narrow, winding track along the high barren cliffs that would appear and then disappear into the rock face. From time to time we passed places that were mined in soviet times to catch out Afghans crossing the river into

Tajikistan. A big rock-fall threatened to inhibit our way but as the men cleared the rubble, we were able to proceed.

We had flown Baltic Air, via Riga, to Dushanbe. In Riga, we fell in with a group of four Englishmen who had been this way before and were, consequently, *au fait* with the strictures of Riga Airport and were very helpful to us. It transpired they worked for an American organization. They were employed installing some very new and innovative security equipment in Dusti, a border town with Afghanistan, in the south of Tajikistan. Complicated to install, this type of x-ray equipment, apparently could detect weapons, drugs, and, so we understood, undesirable people.

We had no booking in the Hotel Poitakht! At least that was what the somewhat grumpy lady receptionist told us when we arrived there at 3.30 am, (well you might be grumpy at that hour). We were tired, despondent and even grumpier, as nobody had been at the airport to meet us. This was despite all the promises and assertions that we would be met by our guide and brought to our hotel. The receptionist desultorily flipped through files, pieces of scrap paper and eventually, as though a vacant room was as rare as hen's teeth, found she had a room she could let us have. Well, at least there was a room, which we immediately accepted. We staggered with our luggage through the gloomy, grey foyer, into the minute lift. Then down a long bare corridor to, amazingly, a suite of rooms. This consisted of a sitting room, bedroom, bathroom and separate lavatory with piping hot water readily available from a huge boiler above the bath. Had we known it at the time, almost all the rooms were vacant despite all the protestations. We were no sooner ensconced than a very young man appeared at our door, introducing himself as Altynbek, our guide. He apologised profusely for having missed us at the airport. Now two elderly European ladies are not hard to pick out in a crowd of mostly young people and Tajiks. We pointed out that perhaps a piece of paper with clients' names on it would be a good idea for future travellers. Anyway, we were most relieved he had turned up, arranging to meet him the following day at 12.30 pm and two not-quite-so-grumpy ladies fell into bed.

Having slept the sleep of the dead until midday, Altynbek, true to his word was waiting for us in the foyer of our soviet type, but clean hotel. He whisked us off for lunch to the The Chaykhona Rokhat, a large, very grand and wonderfully decorative café. He ordered for us, paid the bill and left us to our own devices, which was grand. When we had finished lunch, we drifted along Rudaki, the main thoroughfare, between beautiful old, pastel-painted, neo classical buildings. The street name of 'Rudaki' is in deference to one, Abu Abdullah ibn Mohammad ibn Hakim ibn Abdurrahman ibn Rudaki Samarghandi. He was born in 858 AD in a village in Khorasan (then Persia), now known as Penjikent in Northern Tajikistan. He is regarded as a literary genius and a founder of Tajik-Persian classical literature. As such, Rudaki is highly revered in Tajikistan.

Shaded by trees, a pedestrian path runs down the middle of the street where one can find a bench to sit on and watch the world go by. The girls were mostly dressed in long, bright dresses and pantaloons with matching headscarves or little embroidered pill-box hats. They were tall, with handsome narrow faces, slim straight noses and large dark eyes. Often with a mass of long black hair, sometimes braided, sometimes hanging loose. The men, almost all in Western dress seemed smaller and much less attractive than the girls (barring the manager of the hotel who had eyes to die for).

Unlike Ashgabat, there were lots of shops the most posh being an Adidas shop. New, clean and bright and very western looking, it sported a huge poster offering 40% reductions on goods. We had a look around at the modern fittings and stock but sadly we were the only people there apart from three very pretty attendants who wished us 'good luck'. I think perhaps, they needed the good luck as we left empty-handed.

We had fully intended going to the Museum of National Antiquities right opposite our hotel, but by the time we had had a cup of tea in a nice outdoor café, and sauntered back to the hotel, the museum was closed. Then we realized we had no key and, typically, had forgotten the room number. By great good luck a Tajik teacher of English came to our rescue. She had heard us trying to make ourselves understood to the receptionist. She was most helpful, being only too glad to practice her English. As is our wont – or mine anyway – we found the bar and bought vodka, water and orange juice in preparation for The Big Adventure on the morrow.

Our driver for the following weeks was Altynbek's brother, Asylbek. They were 26 and 29 respectively – almost young enough to be our grandsons. It was into their hands that we trusted our lives! We departed Dushanbe the following morning, passing stalls of melons, apples, tomatoes and big jars of local honey. I noticed one girl wearing a headscarf tied jauntily at the back of her neck like the petals of a great big flower. Frequent police stops curtailed our journey. You know, the little men in the all-important uniform, suddenly becoming little Hitlers. At least once Altynbek had to pay them off. Small tilled fields lined with fruit trees and stands of poplars led to a range of dun-coloured mountains with their heads in the clouds on our left-hand side.

There is a huge trade in goods from China into Tajikistan. For safety and support in times of crises, they mostly travel in convoys of three or four enormous lorries carrying everything from cheap clothes to all sorts of packaged foods. We encountered these behemoths frequently en route churning up clouds of dust as they ground their way inexorably along the terrible roads. About 16 km/10 mi east of Dushanbe, near the village of Obigarm, the tarmac road gradually cracks and disintegrates into a dirt road. Asylbek drove well over the difficult places, but certainly speeded up given a short level stretch. Driving far too fast through villages, scattering children and animals alike and several times he drove over rugs and carpets being scrubbed at the side of the road. We pulled him up on this, pointing out the danger of having a dreadful accident sometime and asked both the boys about motor insurance. Shockingly, but I suppose unsurprisingly, there wasn't any!

The road became more and more rough varying from broken tarmac to rubble. It zigzagged up and up with maybe a 300 m/1,000 ft drop on our right down to the torrent of the River Vakhsh and the partly-built Rogan Dam. In 1993, after heavy rains, the River Vakhsh disintegrated the Rogun Dam which had been under construction for some five years or so. It is now under construction again by the Russians and should eventually bring hydroelectricity to the area. About 85% of Tajikistan's current hydroelectric power is produced by stations along the Vakhsh River. The largest of these is at Nurek. This larger facility at Rogun is unfinished because of lack of financing related to concerns about both security and vulnerability to earthquake. If completed, the Rogan Dam would be the tallest in the world at 335 m/1,105 ft.

Somewhere beyond this area, a bridge had fallen into a tributary river. This necessitated us joining the queue of traffic negotiating a series of hairpin bends on a totally makeshift track. We jolted slowly along, over very unstable, sliding grey scree. Down the steep incline to cross the river at a reasonably shallow place, and up the opposite bank to rejoin the road again. It is a bizarre state of affairs. Somebody with a bit of wit had managed to put up a tiny little sign of an arrow, which is turned around from time to time, indicating a one-way system. This at least warns the huge lorries, so that they don't actually arrive head to head with no possible way of passing each other. Most of the lorries have to take several cuts to enable them to turn the sharp bend at the river's edge. On enquiring, we discovered that most, if not all, of the lorries belonged to the daughter of the President of Tajikistan. To my simple mind, it would seem to make financial sense if the president's daughter forked up the money to build another bridge. Either that, or make a reasonable two-lane road down to and up from the fording place and so facilitating the lorries and all other transport, on their way. At present it is slow and cumbersome, if not downright dangerous This is, after all, the main road in the summer time – the M41 – to the Pamirs and onwards to China.

The scenery however, was stunning. The sun shone brilliantly from a wall to wall blue sky. Gradually the pretty villages became more sparse as we climbed ever higher, the hours ticking away the daylight as we arrived in total darkness at the Khaburabot Pass at a height of 3,252 m/10,500 ft. We were stopped here by border police again, having to show our passports. Then steeply down and down round dozens of hairpin bends. I was quite glad we couldn't see it all in the darkness, and even more glad when we arrived up, somewhere after 8 pm at our guesthouse in Kala-i-Khum.

Almost to our surprise we had beds and were given a very good meal of *plov*. This is a familiar meal to us and a staple of Central Asia. We were also given salad, finishing off with yogurt and local honey. There was a flush toilet and a bath and shower with lashings of hot water, a stroll away from the house, set in a pretty garden full of roses and flowering annuals. A winding path of steps ascended from the back of the garden up the hillside to a viewpoint from where you can see the village, the river – and Afghanistan.

Having left Mirov's house, we drove south along the Panj River – the border with Afghanistan. Then, there was an image that I shall carry with me for ever. Two Afghan men and a little boy, walking along the donkey track on the other side of the river Panj. The river, at this point, was only about 30 m/90 ft across, but they were more than 300 m/1,000 ft above the river. The men carried large loads of grass or perhaps reeds on their backs. They appeared out of what seemed to be a crevasse in the otherwise almost featureless mountainside. Continuing along the tiny track across a rickety bridge, they suddenly saw us watching them from our side of the river. We could see no houses or fields where they might have come from, or proceeded to. Although carrying heavy loads, they walked, not with a laboured tread, but with a buoyant step, stopping to wave to us. Was it their recognition of us, as I watched them through my binoculars, that I found myself overcome with emotion? Or was it because we hear so much about the war in Afghanistan and presume that everybody is caught up in it, so that no-one is able to carry on a normal life? I ought to know better. Although far removed from Afghanistan, we suffered years of civil strife in Northern Ireland. Nobody actually called it a civil war, but it *was* to all intents and purposes – and yet we carried on as usual. My children went to school and we shopped – going through a bag-searching and frisking process – in Belfast. It certainly wasn't nice. But people worked and lived throughout the almost 30 odd years of bombings, shootings and terrible bitterness. And so, I suppose, do most of the Afghanis. Families must be cared for, animals fed, fields tilled and life continued as best possible. Nevertheless, the image of these three people has left its imprint on my memory.

We stopped to buy some fruit at a stall and were almost overtaken by two cyclists. They then stopped having seen that we were European. To our utter amazement, we found ourselves chatting to two Germans on mountain bikes. Two very tough, strong Germans. The girl was young and blond and had legs like a shire horse, not ugly, just strong and muscular. They would need to be on these roads. We had quite a chat with them and asked did they not have numerous punctures. But apparently not. Great bikes and two very determined people. We wished them luck as they whizzed off on their way – at that point, down-hill.

The hotel we stopped at for lunch had apparently always been busy in Soviet times. Now however, it was poor and very run-down. There was no loo and the outdoor pool had no water, but we were able to wash our hands under a hose before lunch. We sat outside on a shady verandah and were entertained by a group of men who were weighing sacks of apricot kernels on a very makeshift weighing machine. After some obvious differences of opinion in regards to the weight of the sacks, everyone seemed to agree on a weight, and price, and money was seen to change hands.

Just beyond the village of Shidz, the Panj broadens out into almost a lake with pale sandy beaches and Afghanistan faded into the distance. At Rushan the Bartang River enters the Panj River just upstream from the town. Bartang means 'narrow passage' (much more on that later). All round Rushan, on this comparatively flattish handkerchief of land, farming was evident from the abundance of poplar and fruit trees, cattle grazing green pastures, and wheat sheaves drying in the sun.

The World's Second Highest Botanical Gardens.
After another long day's drive alongside the Panj River, we arrived in Khorog the principal town of the Gorno-Badakshan (GBAO) region at a height of around 2,100 m/6,500 ft. It has a large market, remarkable botanical gardens, quite a few small inns, a hospital and an extremely good university. We learned that the Aga Khan gave $200,000,000 to establish one of three campuses of the University of Central Asia in Khorog and as a result the town has one of the brightest and best-educated population anywhere in Central Asia.

The town is hemmed in by vertical mountains rising either side of the Gunt River which dashes along, exquisitely clear and bright turquoise blue, yet another tributary of the Panj. Our little inn was again basic but clean and with the luxury of an indoor shower and loo. These were the hardest beds to date, just 'breaking us in' for future beddings, I thought to myself. Although now at over 6000 ft it was still hot. I had been wearing a pair of slip-on mules with bare feet, handy when you have to take off your shoes before entering any of the houses. However, I discovered that between the heat, the dust and the naturally dry climate, I was getting cracked heels, which were quite painful.

Searching through my chemist's shop of toiletries and medications, I discovered a tube of Germolene which I applied liberally and started to wear socks.

We decided we might make a small excursion into the town and have a look around. The Parine Inn where we were staying is up quite a steep hill, so going into town was no problem. We met and tried some conversation with three small girls who were very happy to have their photographs taken. Then we did some shopping at quite a smart looking little shop, which sadly held almost no merchandise at all, barring what we were looking for. This brought us to the river's edge and a park through which we dandered admiring the crystal clear water. On our way back up the hill, huffing and puffing, we passed an elderly (what?) lady carrying some heavy looking bags. She stopped us and opened the bags full of apples and a few pears, obviously wanting us to have one or two. When we tried to pay her for the half dozen or so that we picked out, she was quite diffident about it until we insisted that she take some money, pressing the coins into her hand.

Our driver, Asylbek, had been very quiet all day and in the evening when we went with the boys to quite a swish outdoor restaurant for dinner, he ate almost nothing. Asylbek told us he had very bad toothache. So we said that he must have it attended to there, in Khorog, where there is a hospital and medical services. Otherwise he would have to struggle on to God knows where, where there would be very little help for him. So it was decided that he would go to the hospital early the following morning while we went to the local bazaar.

Without any persuasion, the following morning, Asyl, holding a very swollen face, and having had a miserably sleepless night, took himself off to the hospital situated immediately opposite the market.

The blue-eyed butcher stood below me in the bazaar. I was standing up some steps, on a sort of stone platform, watching him as he cut up a few morsels of meat. He looked up at me, to my surprise through a pair of very blue eyes. I indicated my blue eyes to him and then his and mentioned 'Iskander' (Alexander the Great)

"Da," he replied, "Macedonia." We both laughed.

"Da, da," I replied in my very best Russian. This is yet again, the legend that any blue-eyed people in Central Asia must be descendants from Alexander's armies. However, I think there might possibly have been one or two other blue-eyed people through Tajikistan since 300 BC! I indicated taking his photograph which he at first dismissed. Then when I clenched my hands in a gesture of pleading with him, he nodded but never looked right at me, enabling me to get a couple of great photos. We wandered on through the market passing stall upon stall of Chinese made goods. At last, led by the delicious smell of new-baked bread, we found the bakery and the fruit and vegetable stalls where we bought the makings of a picnic. Delicious fresh bread, tomatoes, cheese and an enormous water melon.

It was only a short walk from the bazaar to the big bridge over the Panj River. Built in 2003 by the Aga Khan Development Trust it is to facilitate the flow of aid into Afghanistan and to encourage commerce and trade. We strolled across it to the other side admiring the structure, but, disappointingly, as it wasn't a market day in Afghanistan, it wasn't open for business.

Asylbek emerged from the hospital smiling sheepishly and holding a handkerchief to his cheek. With the offending tooth removed, he was now out of pain although he made quite an issue over spitting out copious quantities of blood from time to time. He curled up happily in the back seat of the car for a snooze while Altynbek drove us up to the Pamir Botanical Gardens. The second highest in the world they are situated about 5k m/3 mi from the centre of town at 3,900 m/11,000 ft). From the inscription on the sign we learned that the gardens sit on 624 hectares of arable land and house 2,300 plant varieties. The gardens are delightful and pretty impressive. But the further we went the more we began to find that the gardens are a magical, hidden jewel in Tajikistan's rough mountain terrain. We spent a long time walking around looking at the plants, which amazingly seemed to thrive at this altitude. Apparently the area doesn't get too much snow in winter. The last of the summer's long grass, having been cut some days previously, was being pitch-forked as hay up into a wagon for winter fodder. We found a magnificent vantage point for looking down on Khorog, situated on either side of the Gunt River, snaking like a blue ribbon below us.

On our way up to and back from the gardens, I had noticed a group of men working on the road surface. No pneumatic drills in this part of the world. One man was holding a cold chisel and another was attacking it with a sledge hammer in an effort to break the surface. They were making pretty good headway by the time we were coming down, as much of the road had cracked open. Filling the car with petrol is another interesting exercise. There are very few actual petrol stations as we know them, with pumps and hoses. Petrol, or deisel, comes in gerry cans from a lady with a scarf over her mouth and nose, at the side of the road. The fuel is measured out and poured into the car one can at a time. After filling up, Elise and I watched while the three Tajiks – our two boys and the petrol lady – hunkered down on the roadside. After some length of time, having had quite a discussion concerning the price and quantity of fuel, money was again seen to change hands.

About 30 km/18 mi south of Khorog we turned up a side valley. On enquiring, we found out we were going to some hot springs. We followed the road up alongside the river, arriving at the hot springs of Garm Chasma. Here we found a shrine to Ali, the Prophet Mohammed's son-in-law who is reputed to have opened the spring with one stroke of his sword. The spring is quite spectacular. Enormous calcium deposits had, over the years, formed unique sculptures and huge stalacmites. Altynbek went to see if there was a ladies' pool. He cased the joint, finding it difficult to discover anybody who could give him directions.

Then, to his huge embarrassment, he rounded a corner coming face-to-face with the ladies' pool, eliciting a few screams from those concerned. Those concerned were in an outdoor pool at the bottom of a hot waterfall, and, we noticed, were skinny dipping. We pondered over this and decided we would go into the pool but in our cozzies. (Those concerned were young and nubile.) We spent quite a long time enjoying the pool, the nubile girls having been replaced by some rather less nubile.

I suggested we stop beside the Garm Chasma River for our picnic, on the way back down to the main road. Of course we had no such niceties as plates or cutlery. However, with the trusty knife that Elise and I had bought in a market in Majorca, years before, we cut up the tomatoes, cheese and watermelon. We just pulled great chunks from the bread. It was a gorgeous spot shaded by trees as we watched a handful of children on the opposite bank tending a herd of goats. As we had a surplus of watermelon, our boys shouted to the kids asking if they wanted it. 'Does a duck swim?' as they say, or 'Does a boy paddle?' One lad hitched up his trousers, and with great bravado, launched himself into the freezing, swiftly flowing river. We watched with apprehension as, slipping now and then over the rocky bed, he arrived at our side, to receive the half watermelon before safely making the return journey.

Eventually, before us, over the tops of the closer mountains in Afghanistan's Wakhan Corridor, we spied the snowy tops of the Hindu Kush, far away in Pakistan. The strengthening wind, coming from the north behind us, was blowing dust over the river, seeming to hang there like smoke, making the valley look quite surreal. All day, it had seemed to me that we were going downhill. That is, we appeared to have gone down more hills than going up. It must have been a trick of perspective, because the river was always coming towards us – ergo – we had to be going uphill!

A Party in Ishkashim

In Ishkashim, the Wakhan's regional centre and largest village, our night's stay was at Hani's Guest House. We had a very simple white washed room in a house which, when we turned into it off the road, looked frighteningly like a half built factory. The brickwork was the most rudimentary I have ever seen. The concrete bricks just about stuck together with minimal amounts of cement, forming uneven lines, up and down, like waves in the sea. Our accommodation was definitely becoming a bit more basic. We immediately fell into some refreshments, abandoning the idea of a walk. After all, we had had quite a bit of exercise that day, a desultory swim at Garm Chasma and a short stroll along the river at lunch time. We were really fit when we left Ireland, in preparation for great hikes in the Pamirs. So far we had had the odd dander and sat in the car. Mind you, sitting in the car was not just as relaxing as you might think. It was quite a feat of muscular control hanging on for grim death as we hurtled over stones and pot holes and swerved round bends in the road.

Dinner that night was *Laghman* – a sort of Tajik/Irish stew with meat, vegetables and noodles and very good it was with tomato and cucumber salad and green tea. Before leaving home we had sworn we wouldn't eat these salads, as without exception, the handful of people we spoke to who had been to Tajikistan had had really bad tummy trouble. Although we had decided not to eat salads or drink – or even wash our teeth with – tap water, I noticed that we both happily tucked into the salad without a backward glance. As usual the ladies ate separately, the son of the house eating with us. Vali was a charming, good-looking lad who spoke very good English, picked up, so he said, from English-speaking tourists. We learned to our surprise that he was only sixteen. We ended up getting the photos out and showing them to everybody. The ladies were entranced by them and asked if they could keep postcards of Strangford Lough, marvelling at the sea and the green, green fields.

The following day was September 9th, Independence Day in Tajikistan and there was to be a great party in the sports arena. Everyone wanted to partake, so we were persuaded to spend an extra day and night in Ishkashim.

It was a little walk over a dusty path and round a corner from the front door of our B&B to the squat loo, and next door, a bath and shower, similar to that in Khorog. I, personally, have cracked the doubtful delights of 'night visits' when one sometimes has to stagger off in the middle of a dark night to get to the toilet. I have now purchased a Uriwell. It is a small container of corrugated plastic which expands like a concertina and holds lots. I have recommended it to many of my travelling friends.

The next day – September 9th and Independence Day. Vali's mother was the first to leave the house. As well as running the guesthouse she is a teacher in the local school, and had to mind some of the younger children. Elise and I walked later, with Altynbek and Vali, along with everyone else in the vicinity, to the Party in the dusty arena. Here we were entertained with speeches by local dignitaries for some forty minutes or so. During this time we strolled around taking pictures of some of the people. Little girls dressed up in white party frocks with big fluffy bows in their hair and wee boys in smart black suits with ties, all clamoured to have their photographs taken. Happily we found we could get some seats in a small stand. From here, we watched displays of singing and dancing by girls looking very pretty wearing brightly coloured, traditional costume, followed by a smart display of personal, armed combat, by members of the army. It was all quite a long affair, as the sound system kept cutting out interrupting the dancers in mid-pirouette. It was very, very hot and dusty and I had made the fundamental mistake of wearing a fine but black shirt and stupidly forgetting a hat. Clever old Elise had had the forethought to wear a sunhat. We were sitting behind a group of three men, two almost bald, and the third with a head of dark curly hair. As I watched the dancing beyond him, I had to look past his hairy ear. It occurred to me how similar everybody's ears are. Even babies have fully formed ears. Some are bigger and some smaller, some sport sprouts of hair from within, but basically they are the same. I prized my musings away from ears, and returned to the bright and jolly spectacle in the arena below us.

The best fun of the day followed in the afternoon with wrestling matches. One of these got completely out of hand when some of the crowd disagreed with the referee's decision. One onlooker took a poke at the referee, then another and another, until the whole wrestling match turned into a magnificent free-for-all. We avoided the riotous crowd and went to watch a more sedate wrestling match. The Tajiks are rather good at this sort of wrestling, in fact I think it is their national sport. It is a bit like Sumo wrestling. The combatants also try to trip one another up by hooking their feet round the ankles of their opponents. We were quite embarrassed when, as obvious European visitors we were pushed to the front of the circle of spectators. But then we happily joined in with the children and seated policemen for a first class view of the proceedings. We even joined in the cheering for who ever was the favourite with the locals. Each winner received a really good prize. Anything from a sack of grain to a pair of trainers.

After a while we got tired standing, and looked around for somewhere to sit and some shade. The only possible shade was under the roof of the departed 'grandees' little grandstand. As we looked longingly at it, some of the folk already there, waved and beckoned us over. This was great. We were made a great fuss of and yet again, pushed to the front so that we could see the arena. There were a lot of women watching the wrestling, one of whom was the mother of one of the combatants. We shouted and cheered when he won his match and was presented with a huge new thermos flask, which he passed up to his mother. A strikingly good looking woman, she spoke only a very little English, but we got into conversation with a young woman who spoke excellent English and was studying journalism in Khorog University. Then another woman joined in the somewhat confused chat, who told us she was a gynaecologist in the hospital in Ishkashim.

At the end of the wrestling, nothing would do but the gynaecologist lady invited us to her house for tea. As ever, we accepted with alacrity and followed her and a bevy of other ladies, through some streets and into her house. Now, we thought we knew all about Tajik hospitality, but my goodness, we didn't expect just quite so much. Her children excitedly brought sweets, nuts, apricots and little biscuits to the table. Then came copious cups of green tea to be followed by water melon, grapes, damson jam and *kaimak*, that delicious thick clotted cream, and fresh bread. There was also a bowl of dried rosehips, which we were told were good for sore throats. (I remember getting Rosehip Syrup as a child.) Our hostess spoke a little English and was soon joined by her midwife in the hospital also anxious to practise her English. We chatted away as best we could learning much about the plight of women and lack of a voice for women's issues in the government. We were just about to get up and take our leave when we were told that the kebabs were almost ready. Heavens! Cunningly, I said I didn't eat meat and left poor Elise to cope as best she could with the too fresh and very tough meat. But goodness, such kindness and hospitality.

We were eventually able to prize ourselves away, hand-in-hand with the two children and guided back to our B&B. Elise dug out the two tea towels, printed with maps of Ireland, she had thoughtfully brought as presents for just such an occasion, and gave them and some Mars Bars to the girls to take home.

We had noticed on our return, four lads lounging on the divan at the door of the house. Two French and two Dutch. Naturally enough we got talking to them and discovered their car had broken down. Our two boys were helping their driver with the engine but it was obvious they were having to stay the night. They asked had we met an American called Robert during our travels? Yes we had. Both in Khorog and at Garm Chasma hot springs where he had struck both of us as being pretty weird. He had told us he was making a film about the yeti. We were even more amazed, when we saw him later scrabbling about among the minefields beside the road. According to our new young friends he was – not surprisingly – having a lot of trouble with the border guards, his extremely odd sense of humour going totally over their heads. Understandably they had never even heard of a yeti. And in any case, did it come from Tajikistan?

After the hot day, the evening became quite chilly. Elise and I explored round the house, which Vali said was going to be extended into a hotel – crikey! So that is why we thought it looked like a factory. Talking about 'crikey', I obviously say it often, so that one day Altyn asked me, "What does it mean, this word Crikey?"

"Ah," I responded, "I think it is a slang word for Christ."

"Is it permissible then in your religion, to use this word?"

"Oh yes, it's OK, it's not really a very serious slang word," I assured him.

So from then on, when there was anything a bit dangerous, or that needed an expletive, everyone said 'Crikey'. Sometimes, in times of desperation a double crikey!

Elise and I wandered on down through a garden filled with all sorts of vegetables, examining the house's brickwork as we went. We hopped from stone to stone across a little stream, making sure not to come between a cow and her calf, and stood watching as the lowering evening sun shone gold on the snows of the Hindu Kush.

The Wakan Valley.
We were making our way, now in the Wakhan Valley, between Ishkashim and the town of Langar. Still bordered on the right-hand side by the Panj River with Afghanistan and the Hindu Kush beyond. Although dust-dry, everybody from the villages seemed to be busy wielding hook and scythe, harvesting wheat from the tiny fields. Some of the crop was being cut while some stood

already in little stooks drying in the sun. Yet more was being winnowed – separating the grain from the chaff. Stone walls along the roadside and separating the fields were built up to around four feet, then there was a layer of thorny sticks protruding on either side, held in place by the coping stones. What a good idea. The prickly sticks stopped the cattle from pushing the walls over.

The Wakhan Valley, also known as The Wakhan Corridor, is a finger of Afghan territory, running north east to China separating Pakistan and Tajikistan. Created in the 1890s as a buffer zone between the Russian northern territories in Central Asia, and British India (now Pakistan), marking the end of 'The Great Game'.

Khakha Fortress is a splendid ruin on the right-hand side of the road a few miles beyond Ishkashim. Dating back before Islam, it rises from a natural rock platform offering panoramic views across the river and the surrounding area. Khakha is believed to have been the leader of a Zoroastrian tribe that ruled the Wakhan area, but was defeated around the time of the area's conversion to Islam. We made a good exploration of the summit, taking care not to go too near the Afghan side, which was presently occupied by Tajik border guards. A little further along the road is an Ishmaeli tomb, said to be that of Ali, Mohammed's son-in-law.

For a time, and most unexpectedly, our road surface improved into being reasonably smooth. Perversely, Asyl slowed down to a crawl, which was great going through a village, but incredibly irritating in the countryside. Most of the time we would be driving through a dry, almost colourless landscape. But now and then, we crossed little bridges over blue, gin-clear, sparkling streams, bordered by banks of grasses, herbs and flowering shrubs – tiny oases of vegetation and colour.

Hurray, hurray! At last we could see the white, twin peaks of Marx and Engels – the famous mountains of the High Pamirs – in the distance. They appeared in front of us, beyond the dusty hills, laced together by our once again wobbly road appearing and disappearing round the contours. About a mile after Ptup village we turned left up a tortuous zig-zag track, disturbing flocks of hoopoes, fluttering away from our approaching vehicle. It seemed as if we might fall off the mountain the track was so steep, climbing ever upwards. And then, round a corner we came to rest at the 3rd to 1st century BC, Yamchun Fort, perched high on a ridge, complete with round watch-towers and outer walls. Situated across a steep gully from where we stood, it was most dramatic. We decided it was probably the most impressive fortress either of us had ever seen. It would have been good to have visited it but the harsh terrain between us and the fort looked too daunting. So we abandoned that idea and plumped instead for the softer option of continuing on up the track to the Bibi Fatima Hot Springs.

Named after the Prophet Mohammed's sister, this spring is reputed to increase women's fertility. Well, I don't think either of us were in need of that. But as usual, we were curious enough about saunas, banyos and hot springs to take a look. We were brought into a small humid, ante-room, which in turn, as far as we could see, gave onto a flight of steps going down into a pool. After the bright sunlight outside, it took a minute or two for our eyes to adjust to the darkness. Outside, down the steps, a river fell in a sparkling torrent over mossy green rocks and into a narrow pool. It was dark and eerie. But nothing daunted, we stripped off, and with some trepidation descended a ladder into the dark, womb-like pool, immersing ourselves into the warm, swirling water. Elise tried taking a few pictures but of course with the humidity the camera misted up, resulting in hazy photographs. When we eventually finished our bathe and exited the little building, we met up with a man who was directing some excavations. A small digger was moving earth up a very steep hill. We had to scramble over piles of rock and debris while the digger continued to work at a most perilous angle, hurling rocks and stones towards us. The man told us they were making a road further up the valley to build a hotel behind the hot springs. Another hotel, well I never.

Well well, a few miles after Ptup and back again on the main road, who should we see there, on the side of the road, but our Dutch and French chums. They were visiting the Pamiri house of a Sufi mystic, astronomer and musician called Mubarak Kadam who died about 1930. We stopped also, having heard that the house was well worth a visit. It was indeed beautiful, with carved poplar-wood beams and pillars, and round the square sky-light. The four intricately carved ceiling squares, represented the four elements of earth, water, air and fire. In the main room was a collection of the mystic's musical instruments, some of his books and clothes. All this, lovingly cared for by a local man living nearby. He took us to see the solar calendar, which had been used to calculate the spring and autumn equinoxes. We admired everything, including an apricot tree, simply laden with fruit and suggested we might buy some. Of course this was a fine idea, but we were going to have great difficulty doing justice to the enormous bag of very ripe apricots which he presented us with.

The boys had asked us whether we were going to take a look at a Buddhist stupa at Vrang. Of course never to be out-done we said we would and set off down the road. On arrival at Vrang, we found we needed to climb quite a steep hill. I donned my boots and off we went, wading wetly over a little stream. We were guided on our way by an enthusiastic small boy, incongruously wearing a dark suit and tie – apparently straight from school. Up we climbed along an almost non-existent, very steep path of very slippery shale. Each footstep sent a mini-avalanche down to the valley below. Elise, frightened she might join the avalanche, was a bit dubious about continuing. Just at this minute, we heard a high mewing above us, sounding I thought, like a buzzard only to be told they were choughs. We watched these big birds for a few minutes – just long enough to give ourselves a breather. I didn't mind the path so much. It was my lack of puff that let me down. But we don't give in too easily. The stupa, when you get there, provides a wonderful view of the surrounding country. They say it is possibly of Zoroastrian origin, the land around it showing the remains of fire-worshipping platforms.

What a busy and very interesting day with, at last, lots of exercise. However, our exercise for the day wasn't finished yet. We arrived at our homestay in Langar, a tiny village of about 800 souls, and immediately asked to see the toilet before it became dark. We were taken down two or three steps, through a gateway and on down 200 or so yards along a very rough path to a little tin gate in the fence of a vegetable plot. Along a mud path to a kazi and, at last, the anticipated 'long-drop' (So this is why the cabbages were growing so well) and, I thought, from now on most assuredly, the order of the day. It was of course OK during the day, but in the middle of the night? I don't think so. Back at the house we were shown our room. The walls were entirely covered with rich red patterned carpets. I admired this attractive sort of insulation, keeping the room cooler in summer and warmer in winter. The ceiling sported an ornate, five-lamp chandelier but holding just one low voltage bulb keeping the room very dark.

We sat for a while during our cocktail hour on a bench outside reading and writing, until it became too dark. A bit before 7 pm we headed in to the dish of spuds we had ordered for dinner. The potatoes here were delicious so we were happy enough and added lashings of *kaimak* for a very tasty dish.

The Khargush Pass, at 4344 metres, which I worked out to be a little over 14,000 feet, is quite disappointingly flat. There are, however, two flashing brilliant turquoise-blue lakes – full of birds – in the otherwise drabness of the mountains. We descended from the car and were immediately struck by the wonderful view behind us, back to the Koh-i-Pamir massif in Afghanistan. As we wandered off to take a closer look at the lakes in bright sunshine, we were also struck by the thin air at this height and the bitterly cold wind.

We had left Langar early in the morning noticing that we passed many herds of sheep being driven downhill to winter pastures. Several times we were amused to see young calves or baby kids being given a lift on the backs of donkeys. We were annoyed with Asyl again as he was so impatient, hooting the horn continuously and banging the side of the car trying to move the animals. It was ridiculous. You can't make animals stay at the sides of the road to let cars pass, it takes a little time and anyway, they belonged here.

From Langar to Khargush we were still alongside the same Panj River as the border with Afghanistan. But it was now called the Pamir River, which flows from Zor Kul Lake. The first European known to have visited the lake was the British naval officer John Wood in 1838. Named after the then Queen of England, the lake became known to the British as Lake Victoria of the Pamirs. The lake was thought to be the source of the Oxus, but in fact, the source is the melt water from massive glaciers which run into Zor Kul Lake. At the town of Khargush, we went left, heading northwards; finally, after so many miles, leaving behind Afghanistan. Heading now for the pass and to the village of Bulankul and Lake Yashil Kul. To our surprise, a little before Bulankul we hit the Pamir Highway again, what a joy to be driving on tarmac! It wasn't of course to last as we took off down a side road to Bulankul and the lake.

Bulankul, Ashikul and the Petroglyphs.
The cold, grey, wind-swept bleakness of Bulankul and its apparent abject poverty came as a sharp reminder that we were now in eastern Tajikistan. Here, the mountains of the High Pamirs – the Roof of the World – cover approximately 97% of the land, and where many people barely scratch a living. I looked around shaking my head in dismay as I took it all in. The dust and sand blew around every corner of the rough little stone-built houses. Old tyres and broken-down lorries littered the place. Some small sheds sheltered a few donkeys and goats. However, a good big pile of cow-dung pancakes stood ready for the approaching winter's fires when, we were told, the temperature can fall to a grim minus 52 degrees. We noticed particularly, an aging lady, who hobbled along with the aid of a stick to pick up pats of cow-

dung off the ground, which she put in her bucket. Then she trudged laboriously to a small seat where she sat, head down – the very picture of dejection. However, as usual, the children came to look at us and yet again were very keen to have their photographs taken. We photographed them playing in an old cart which they had made into a sort of playpen, Elise lifting up the littler kids too small to climb up. After a while we were called into a house for lunch where we ate bony but delicious fish called *osmon* caught in the lake by our host. I'm not very good with bony fish but did my best with them. Altyn looked with horror at all that I had left and asked me did I not want any more. As I shook my head, he proceeded to nibble and suck every last morsel off the bones. Nothing would be wasted.

It is a three hour hike there and back, to see Lake Yashil-Kul meaning 'green lake'. In fact, the colour was a superb blue – an immaculate reflection of the sky. The lake nestled between low brown hills, the late growth of grass, cut and piled into small haystacks round the shoreline. Three hours is just about our limit at this altitude – downhill fine, but uphill – really tough going.

We noticed the small, thin man trying to hitch a lift on the side of the road as we approached the village of Alichur. We were speeding along again, back once more on the Pamir Highway. Huge Chinese lorries, also speeding along, on their way back and forth between China and Dushanbe, were roaring past this man, completely ignoring his existence. We turned off to the right, ending up at a homestay and yurt. We were given the choice of staying in an ordinary room in the house, or inside the family yurt. The owner, an attractive, tall, slim lady dressed in a long maroon striped coat and matching head scarf, proudly showed us the yurt. Her long narrow face, full lips and high cheek-bones suggested a Kyrgis background of which we would see many in the days to come. There was no competition. Even though we would be sleeping on the floor and the 'long-drop' was behind a blue door a 100 m/110 yd away – the yurt won hands down. We admired the yurt's beautiful wall-hangings made by the owner's mother and mother-in-law and heated by a dung-burning stove in the centre of the floor. A recce of the village didn't take too long. A white-painted school and little mosque stood out as being the newest buildings in the town. But, as we walked along by the river, yet another broken bridge was symptomatic of the lack of money, and perhaps, also, enterprise.

Meanwhile, back at the yurt, we discovered our four European friends, plus the small, thin hitch-hiker from the side of the road. As it was getting towards the twilight hour, it was not going to be possible for any of them to venture further until the morrow, so they all decided they would like to come and stay with us! To the extent that the four young men wanted to share our yurt with the hiker, in exchange for the two-man room in the house. "Not on your life," we remonstrated, feeling rather mean. "We got here first." Luckily they were all able to find other lodgings in the village, which made us feel not quite so selfish. The hitcher came to visit us later to ask if he could possibly take a lift with us to Murghab the following day. It was fine by us so long as our two chaps concurred. The hitcher, Kabir, was an Indian Sikh by birth but was now an Australian citizen from Perth. He came and offered us a Yoga session when he came to thank us for the lift the next day. Isn't it great the people you meet travelling – but so far, nobody remotely *near* our age.

I woke early the following morning having slept badly. The higher we got the worse I slept. I also had really vivid dreams when I did sleep, so my mind was as busy during the night as the day. Although my body was toasting warm when I woke, I could feel that my face was cold and surmised that it might well be frosty outside. At about 6 am the lady of the house came quietly into the yurt to stoke up the fire using a very sweet-smelling scrubby bush called *Teresken*. It lit up immediately, crackling merrily and in no time at all the yurt was warm again.

We set off quite early with our new Indian friend tucked into the back of the car among the bags. We could see that it had, indeed, been frosty during the night. The morning sun, for the first time was hazy, struggling to bring its now familiar warmth from behind some thin swirling clouds. The area round Alichur is supposed to be quite fertile and certainly around our homestay the fields were tilled and again wheat was being harvested. But farther on up the road towards Murghab it became barren and stony with a complete dearth of vegetation.

Still on the Pamir Highway and some 64 km/40 mi beyond the turn-off for the village of Bash Gumbaz, we suddenly took a right turn onto a barely discernible track. So far as I could see, in the middle of absolutely nowhere. Obviously Asyl was familiar with the area as he drove the car in a series of twists and turns into the desolate, but rather beautiful and dramatic Kurtiskei Valley. We were here to see the ancient Shakhty petroglyphs. These were only discovered in 1958 by some Soviet geologists who had scrambled up a slope to shelter in a cave, only to find the following morning these beautifully preserved cave paintings, dating back to Neolithic times. And here we were preparing to scramble up the same slope. "It's easy," said our boys. "You don't need to put on boots." How stupid of me to heed their advice. We set off, Kabir almost running up the skree slope in front of us. It wasn't too bad to start with, but at an altitude of around 3,963 m/13,000 ft (and getting higher by the second) and in a pair of mules, it was not just a walk-in-the-park. However, we made it and were rewarded with the wonderful red-ink paintings of a bear hunt, still perfectly legible on the cave wall. I turned round to look back from whence we had come to be greeted with the stunning panorama of the valley beneath me. Our large car reduced to the size of a toy. Across the deserted valley floor, the colours of the rock strata were muted shades of greys, browns, creams and pinks.

A Wild-East Town
How does one describe Murghab? The Lonely Planet calls it a 'Wild-East-Town' – a perfect description. At 3,576 m/11,600 ft,

its small population of around six and a half thousand, live in a dry, dusty bowl surrounded by mountains. The shops along the main street are made from discarded containers and a market of small stalls displayed meagre quantities of fruit and vegetables. Any of the houses lucky enough to be on the electricity grid enjoy the alternate days of doubtful and intermittent electricity. This is of such a low voltage that the lighting is almost imperceptible – recharging batteries is a definite no-no. The town positively bristles with telegraph poles, erected for use during Soviet times but now, I think, totally redundant. However, being now so close to the border with China, on almost every day, before the wind gets the dust blowing, there is a fine view of the 7,546 m/24,757 ft snowy peak of Mustagh Ata. We had passed by Mustagh Ata some years previously on our way from the Kunjerab Pass to Kashgar. Our home-stay up above the town, this time had one bed in our room. I did wonder whether we were supposed to share it! But I grabbed the floor – spreading my stuff with a deftness born now of habit, as quick as a flash establishing my 'patch'. As we had arrived in Murghab around lunch-time we decided to dine out in this, the boys' home town. They knew the lie-of-the-land and the best hot spot in town where we enjoyed another meatless *plov*. It was all fine and as ever served by a fascinated, smiling and attentive staff.

Both Elise and I felt the need to do a bit of exploring on our own and in any case wanted to do a few messages. So we bid our boys farewell, assuring them we would find our way back to our B&B and set off to suss out the shopping possibilities. Around half the population in Murghab is Kyrgys we noticed from the quite different facial features and the tall white felt hats worn by the men. We tried several of the 'container' shops, looking for a pen of any sort for me and tissues for Elise. Success on the first count. This, from a helpful shopkeeper who had papered the walls of his container, converting it into quite a cosy little shop carrying a selection of sundry items – but no tissues. Tissues must be unheard of here as we were not able to find them at all. Instead, Elise bought some coarse, brown toilet paper, which she reckoned she could use as a tissue if desperate. We wandered along the row of vegetable stalls, choosing some rather good grapes, some tomatoes and an enormous watermelon, which are always good. Back in our lunchtime restaurant, we had a most amusing time trying to describe orange *koc* (pronounced "sock"). They understood *koc* as it is Russian for juice, but orange was beyond them. In fact I don't think they knew that such a thing as orange juice even existed, and we had to settle for apple *koc* instead.

Armed with our booty, we climbed the hill back to our homestay, deposited our shopping and went off to take a look at The Yak House. This is a showroom and shop attached to the Murghab Ecotourism Association (META) office. It was quite a stiff walk, but interesting when we got there. The building is attractive and very cleverly designed, incorporating the architectural elements of both a yurt and a traditional Pamiri house. There is a small museum and an internet café as well. The little shop offered all sort of handcrafts made by local women. We both bought some small purses and earrings for Elise. As ever in Central Asia, there were some beautiful rugs for sale but much too bulky and heavy for us to bring home. We suggested that it would be a good idea to have smaller items for sale. Woven belts, small pictures, and any sort of jewellery are always good souvenirs as they are small and easy to carry.

I had had the idea previously of asking our boys if it would be possible to see and hear local musicians, on one of the two evenings we would be in Murghab. So we were delighted, on our return to the house, when they informed us that yes, it would be possible. The musicians were available that very night and would cost us $30 each. We said to go ahead and book them and to see if they could find our Dutch and French chums. We knew they were also in Murghab, and thought we would invite them to come along for the concert. The response was positive, the four young men being rather diffident to start with, as they couldn't afford to pay. We were going to pay anyway and it made a much better audience, so we insisted they come along.

We had no idea what a 'bucket shower' was, but had been told whatever it was, we could have it. So in fractured English with lots of miming we asked if we could have one. Looking a little doubtful, the daughter of the house disappeared off, only to reappear about an hour later. She beckoned me to follow her across the yard, and into an out-house, which in turn gave into another room. They were all breathtakingly hot from a stove in one corner heating a huge basin of water. I returned for Elise and along with our dirty clothes we hurried off for yet another new type of ablution. As well as the big basin of roasting hot water, there were several other bowls, pans and buckets of cold water. We had a wonderful time with lots of laughter, taking it in turns to stand in a pan of hot water, tramping our "smalls" underfoot in the shampoo from our washed hair. I relished the delicious feeling of bowls-full of clean, hot water as it flowed down my body, washing away the grey dust to mingle with the grey water from the dirty clothes under my feet.

It was becoming really cold now in the evenings as we sat in our darkening room, hoping someone would give us a fire. Indeed they did. We watched in fascination as several members of the family came into our room with a new chimney pipe for the stove. They attached it onto the back of the stove and then had to wiggle it about to slot it up into the hole in the roof. Several twigs and a couple of matches and bingo, within a few minutes we had a roaring fire. We laughed as we strung up Elise's expandable clothes line, attaching our clean clothes over the stove, looking for all the world like a Chinese laundry.

Elise had been talking about a strange sensation of tingling in her hands every so often, but both of us were well and neither could think of an explanation for her complaint. Until now, when she said she had been taking medication for altitude sickness, and on reading the instructions, discovered that tingling in the fingers was one of the side effects. "Elise," I said, "you don't get altitude sickness, I was the one in Peru who got sick."

"I know," she said, "but I thought that perhaps I had something wrong with my heart as I get this thumping on and off."

"Well," says I, "it's when you don't get the thumping that you need to worry." She decided that she seemed to be OK and would stop taking the medication.

The evening concert was a great success. We had had to scramble about tidying up and tidying down the washing line. The four lads turned up, very grateful that we had asked them along, apologising that they could only afford a tip for the musicians. There was a handsome man in a tall white hat who played the accordion and sang songs that he had written. A girl who played a three-stringed instrument – a *tanbur,* which she plucked rather than bowed. And a second girl who sang and danced, encouraging us to dance along with her. It was an hour's delightful entertainment, all taking place in our bedroom.

Our bedroom window faced east, so, in the morning, as soon as the sunshine spilled over the mountain range beyond the town, it poured into the room and onto where I slept ensuring my wakefulness. As I turned over, my hair fell, with its newly-washed softness, like a curtain, shielding my eyes from the bright rays. The mornings were always glorious – cloudless, windless, clear and warm. A heavenly start to each day.

Phsart and Madyan Valleys and more Hot Springs.
What a pity we are so bloody old! Otherwise we would have had a go at the hike from the Gumbezkol Valley, about 9 km/5.5 mi up to the 4,731 m/14,000 ft odd Gumbezkol Pass and another 7 km/4 mi down into the Madiyan Valley. They say it is about a half day's hike, but even giving it a day, we decided we weren't quite fit enough to do it at this altitude. Nevertheless, we drove down the Pshart Valley to the start of the Gumbezkol Valley, and to the yurt and its owner, Shamsky. This elderly Kyrgis gentleman greeted us warmly, inviting us into his yurt. Asleep, totally

covered over, in a rocking cradle was his grandson, while his daughter went about the business of making tea on the yak-dung-fuelled stove. Our host talked non-stop. He was possibly unaware that we couldn't understand a word. Then suddenly, and without any warning, he burst into song. Word perfect, he sang 'Twinkle Twinkle Little Star'. We were delighted and amazed. Shamsky told us he was 70, so he would have been educated by the Soviets. How he came to know the nursery rhyme we couldn't discover. We were to stay the night here in his yurt while he would stay in with his daughter. To our surprise, Asylbek asked whether it would be OK if he and his brother slept with us. Wow, you don't get an offer like that every day! However Elise, was unamused by my effort at humour, and absolutely horrified, declared certainly not. My sailing experiences have inured me to the doubtful 'joys' of sleeping with whoever is on the boat. So it doesn't faze me too much having to sleep with members of the opposite sex – it is, after all, simply sleeping. But, I did agree with Elise, particularly at our age, I don't think it should be necessary to share accommodation with the guide and driver. So we said we didn't think it was a good idea and could they find somewhere else to sleep.

The walk up the Gumbezkol Valley was delightful and fairly easy going, over yellow withered grass. Small flowering plants nestled between rocks as we followed a little stream, which, as we ascended, became icy at its edges. Gradually, after a couple of hours, we approached the snow line – quite deep snow here and there. At times the sun would go behind a cloud, the wind would pick up and it would become really cold. We could see how much further we would have had to go if we had been going to the pass. It was still quite far, and getting steeper and snowier all the time. To be honest, we were glad we were not going 'over the top'. After lunch we explored the Ak Jylga valley on the other side of the Pshart Valley. I found this a much harder climb, stony and rough and much, much steeper, having to cross and re-cross the river which ran down from the heights above us. We passed a herd of plump, healthy-looking yaks being driven down to the pastures below. And then Altyn, who had been carrying my binoculars, spied a large herd of ibex up a gorge opposite us. These were probably Siberian Ibex, the species that live in Central Asia and Russia. Sizes and weights vary greatly but males can reach nearly 300 lb. Both males and females are light tan or brown and both have beards. Although the females' horns are quite small, the mature male can grow magnificent horns up to 130 cm/51 in. They are all as sure footed 'as a mountain goat', living in the high reaches of the mountains.

It was very exciting. The boys encouraged us to hurry up and try and get a bit nearer. We set off, the boys almost at a run, Elise going pretty well while I, as usual, brought up the rear, until I thought my heart would burst! We did get a bit nearer, but of course, just as we thought we might get a photo with the zoom, we must have spooked the ibex, which, with extraordinary agility took off up the rocky gorge and out of range. A bit disappointing, but nevertheless a wonderful experience to have seen them at all, so well camouflaged against the mountainous backdrop.

Back down at the yurt we passed what was left of the evening before dark, watching the yaks being milked while Shamsky carried his grandchild around on his back, talking incessantly to us. We all decided he wasn't 'quite the full shilling' and Elise and I started feeling a bit apprehensive about the night in the yurt. Already we felt guilty at putting the old man out of his home, but, even more, would he forget he was staying with his daughter and come bumbling in to visit us? As though he could read our thoughts, Asylbek suggested to Elise that perhaps we should return to our homestay in Murghab for the night. Without a moment's hesitation, she agreed, the thought of the flesh-pots of Murghab being too attractive to decline.

The drive back in the dark up the Pshart Valley was hair-raising. So we were much relieved to arrive at our little restaurant for fried eggs and a beer, and thence to our nice friendly B&B, the hot stove, and bed.

The Madyan Valley is situated south and then west of Murghab. We followed the Murghab River into the valley, which has to be one of the prettiest places in the area. The river gently meanders along the wide valley floor, flowing either side of little islands of trees, bushes and greenery – the first we had seen for days. Small birds and butterflies abounded and at one little oasis, we watched some ducks a-dabbling. Gradually the valley and the river narrowed, the river becoming faster. The walls of the valley closed in exposing strange rock formations, resembling dripping, wet toffee which had become hardened. We walked on until we came to some more petroglyphs having to dodge over and around small trees and lots of wild flowers. What a perfect place for a picnic, sitting on the river bank, cooling our feet and the water bottles and washing tomatoes in the cold, clear river. The Murghab River continues on upstream, joining the Pshart River, flowing out of Sarez Lake. This 60 km/35 mi long lake was formed in 1911. During an earthquake, half a mountain slid down into the valley plugging the Murghab river and obliterating villages. Gradually the lake filled up to 500 m/1860 ft behind the dam of rocks and mud, the highest dam in the world – natural or man-made. If another quake damaged the Usoi Dam – named after one of the buried villagers – and the waters of the lake escaped, destruction on a horrific scale would ensue.

After our walk and leisurely lunch, the Madyan Hot Springs beckoned. Even if we weren't able to have bucket showers, the easy availability of natural springs would keep even the most fastidious traveller happy. Over another rickety-looking bridge and up another cork-screwing excuse for a track, we arrived at Eli Su and the hot springs. Two families live here looking after the bath house and two large green-houses growing tomatoes and cucumbers. The greenhouses had been donated by a German well-wisher, heated by both the sun and geo-thermally, supplying vegetables both for the families and for sale in Murghab.

The 'Bathhouse Lady' took us to one of two little wooden huts where she showed us the pool. Happily we undressed and approached the water. Squealing in dismay, Elise withdrew her foot from the scalding water. "It's almost at boiling point," she said. She tried again and again but simply could not get into the water.

"Let's have a go," I offered, and managed to keep my feet in for an instant. Gradually, I was able to stand in the water and splash myself, like old women do at the seaside – this was a lot hotter than the seaside. It really was too hot to handle. Annoyed with ourselves for not being able to bear the water, we got dressed and exited the bathroom. Totally perplexed, our hostess laughed when we mimed 'too hot'. Where then, was Altyn? In the hut next door. Obviously un-fazed by the heat, he emerged some time later, pink-faced and glowing. I had been sitting beside the lady watching the interplay between her, her daughter and grand-daughter. It could have been my family. Granny absently and tenderly stroking the little girl's arm while the child cuddled her Mum, pulling her cheeks into funny grimaces. I suddenly suffered a wave of home-sickness and later, on Elise's phone, managed to get a call through to my daughter at home.

I again slept badly that night, finally giving up around 5ish, lying quietly for a while then reading for a bit. Eventually, giving up all hope of going back to sleep, I got up and dressed around 7.30 – Elise still asleep. On my way out I bumped into the two friendly younger daughters of the house as they left for school. The morning was again beautiful, still chilly but calm and bright. We had had several nights here in Murghab and although the town is poor and dusty, our homestay was as good as conditions allowed. We got our fire made up sometime after 6 o'clock each evening when it gets really chilly and we were able to boil water on the stove for either a Cup-a-Soup or a coffee. Without language in common it was frustrating not to be able to communicate better. Then we discovered that the older daughter of the house, Fatima Sheralina, who worked in an office, but was on maternity leave, spoke a little English. We were constantly amazed at the number of people who could speak some English in this far-removed part of Asia. Fatima told us she was 28, and had her new little daughter, Asel, having lost a baby son some years previously. While we were staying in the house, the family stayed in their yurt in the yard. That was, Granny, mother and father, Fatima and Asel and a couple of younger sisters. Fatima's husband, Mendebi, lived away all summer tending the yaks in the high pastures. So, I wondered, how do these people conduct their love lives? Much the same, I suppose, as 60 years ago in the west of Ireland, although the cottages there mostly had two rooms. Is it just a necessary bodily function for the men and a rather pleasureless experience for the women through which they become pregnant? I can't really imagine flailing around in the throes of ecstasy with Granny looking on. I tried vaguely to broach the subject with Fatima and later with Altyn, but it became too embarrassing all round to actually get down to the nitty-gritty of it, so, as yet, it remains an unanswered question.

Life for everyone up in the High Pamirs is unimaginable to us. Almost everyone is involved in animal husbandry but the land is so poor – arid and stony – that it is hard even to grow enough fodder for the winter. There is a large flat area of land outside Murghab, which was reserved by the Soviets, solely for hay and winter fodder. Nowadays, everyone uses it during the summer with the result that there isn't enough grass left over for hay-making. Fuel is a huge problem. The local brushwood – *Teresken* – is an ancient, slow-growing, staple fodder plant with a huge root system which is being torn up by its roots for fuel so it cannot regenerate and is slowly disappearing. A plant of 30 cm/39 in or so might well be 50 to 80 years old. Some coal is imported from Kyrgistan. We did notice, however, that many houses and even the yurts have solar panels on the roofs, supplying energy, even if only a little for lighting. It's heating in the cold winters that is a problem. Almost everyone we spoke to – that is, the man in the street – regretted the passing of the Soviet Era when everything seemed to be better.

Tourism of course might bring in some much-needed cash, but the infrastructure needs so much improvement. So far, we have only met 10 other travellers, none of them British or Irish, all years younger than us and all but one – men. At present travelling is hard. The food most of the time is unappetising to Europeans, especially at altitude where one loses one's appetite anyway. The home-stays are fine, but very basic and mostly sleeping on the floor. Our hosts, however, without exception, have been so pleasant, thoughtful and hospitable that one is nearly killed with kindness. But then... there is the lavatory long-drop system. Squat loos, usually at a fair distance from the house or yurt, and for older folk that would be by far the biggest problem. In this area of the Pamirs, we were most of the time somewhere around 4,000 m/12,000 ft. But despite many dispiriting prognoses from other travellers, barring a slight headache to begin with, we soon became acclimatised and felt healthy and well. META, the Murghab Ecotourism Association, created by the French Non-governmental Association ACTED, is doing an enormous job in promoting independent travel in the Pamirs. It provides information linking together locals interested in tourism with travellers. The organisation can offer home stays, yurt stays, drivers, guides and even camel owners for hire to tourists and trekkers at reasonable prices.

As I mentioned earlier, a great deal of excellent work is done through the Aga Khan Foundation. We found that the people of both northern Pakistan, Kyrgistan and Tajikistan revere him with almost every home displaying his portrait.

Karakul and We Lose Our Bottle
Time to move on and leave the relative refinements of Murghab. We were headed north over the 4,655 m/15,118 ft – Akbaital Pass, to Lake Karakul and the village of the same name. Most tourists head on from Karakul north again over the Kyzylart Pass on the border of Kyrgistan, onwards to Sary Tash and Osh from

where you can fly to a variety of places. We however, having been to Osh, have plumped to complete our circumnavigation of the High Pamirs, by returning to Dushanbe via the very remote Bartang Valley.

We set off on the amazingly well-surfaced road out of Murghab, climbing gradually with great views of the snowy slopes of Mustagh Ata in China. Passing the turn-off to Rangkul where we would have liked to visit, but lack of time prohibiting us, we continued straight on. High mountain tops to our left, glittering white against the perfect azure sky.

The last kilometre or so up to the pass was steep and dramatic. We stopped of course, getting out of the car to take some photographs. There, on the other side of the road was a beaten-up old Toyota, with two people trying to light a fire. Inquisitive as usual, Elise and I wandered over to where they were. "We're trying to discover how long it takes to bring water to the boil at this altitude," spoke the woman.

"Oh yes," I countered, "we did this some years ago in Tashkurgan in China, and although the water seemed to boil, it wasn't very hot."

The couple were, again Dutch. The Dutch, for all their small country, seem to be good travellers. They had driven from Holland and were continuing on to Mongolia! We were astonished that they were attempting these mostly appalling roads in an ordinary saloon car, which was certainly not in its first bloom of youth. They were a great deal more mad then us, I thought. Anyway, we bid each other good luck and continued on our merry way.

Steeply down the north side of the pass, scattering marmots as we went and almost scattering two cyclists, tearing flat-out downhill in front of us. Double Crikey! There is a wide neutral, mountainous zone including part of the Sarykol Range between Tajikistan, and China. But just to be on the safe side that no one would be tempted to illicitly cross from one country to the other, there is a 2 m/7 ft high barbed-wire fence running along the Tajik border, parrallel with our road. It seemed so pathetic a barrier. This huge, wild landscape reducing the fence's redoubtable strength into a mere triviality. About 40 km/25 mi from the pass are the ruins of a Russian Tzarist post, which was later used by the Red Army against the *basmachi* rebels. Marco Polo passed this way in 1274AD, and the explorer/adventurer, Francis Younghusband came to have a look in the early 1880s. Down and down, then round a bend and before us, Lake Karakul, created by a falling meteor around 10 million years ago. Flanked on either side and beyond by range after range of snow-topped mountains. Mauves, greys, slate-blues and the lake of turquoise steaked with lapis lazuli. It was yet another breathtaking sight in this most extraordinary country.

Our home-stay in the village was similar to those we had already stayed in. We were given a large, empty room furnished with a stove. It was about lunch time so Elise and I enjoyed a Cup-a-Soup and some bread and yogurt. The long-drop here was miles away from the house – well, some distance anyway. Through a big gate, along a rough path, up a flight of uneven steps and there it was – far too far away for night visits. Also staying here were yet another four Dutch, VSO Aga Khan workers from Khorog. A stunning, tall, blond girl called Hettie and her husband and two other men – all medical workers.

After lunch, Elise and I went to explore along the lake shore. We walked down to the water's edge, via the village dump, where to our astonishment we discovered a couple of pairs of the huge twisted horns of the 'protected' Marco Polo sheep. Upon remarking about this later to Altyn, he said the sheep were hunted and slaughtered regularly by the villagers. Why not? They were abundant in the area and made very good eating. We had been told that the lake was salty, but on tasting it, it hardly tasted salty at all. In any case, it freezes over in winter and is too high to support any life. We meandered on towards some sort of an abandoned building on the near horizon. Upon reaching it, we found several buildings, all in a state of disrepair, roofless and windowless. We spent some time exploring around, supposing they had been Soviet buildings as I had picked up an ancient Soviet army button. Later we learned it had been an army sanatorium.

We returned by way of the village. More dry, dusty, colourless streets linking small square houses. No sign at all of a shop. A few children were running about – one boy proudly rode round and round on a bike.

Back at the B&B about cocktail hour, I went to pour us a drink. Where was the drinks bag? We searched and searched. I knew I had brought it out of our room in Murghab and thought it had been put into the back of the car. Searched the car back and front – and middle. No booze bag. Disaster and dismay. Not only had we lost the vodka which we thought would be replaceable, but tragically, Elise's Jameson whiskey. Also my nice little beakers and Elderflower cordial from home. We sent Altyn and Asyl off to do a recce of the village to track down some vodka. Not only were there no shops, there was no vodka either. Alas and alack, we would have to be TT for the night. Our hostess and a child of about ten came in to make up our beds. This little girl was amazing. She worked away all evening making the visitors comfortable and in the morning tidied up after us. A far more responsible and helpful child than any ten-year-old at home.

The night? Now that was interesting. To start with, the young woman who ran our homestay was worried about her very young baby. She and Altyn asked Elise if they could borrow the car to take the baby the 40 km/25 mi back to Murghab to have her examined. However, Elise said that the Dutch lady was a midwife and perhaps she would help. This was a much better idea as she was on hand and was very happy to be of assistance. The mother and baby, and Hettie the medic, came into our room asking if they could examine the baby as it was private and warm. Altyn came to translate. It seemed that the baby, who had been breast-feeding normally and regularly had started crying a lot. The Mum had already lost one baby and was upset and worried that she might lose another. I held a torch for better light while they stripped the baby and Hettie examined her very carefully finding nothing wrong. She thought perhaps the baby, as it grew bigger, was hungrier and suggested the Mum tried feeding her more often. There is absolutely no medical or maternity help of any sort in Karakul other than having to go to Murghab, or Osh, over the border in Kyrgistan. It really impinged on me that here, it absolutely is, survival of the fittest.

(According to a WHO online database, in 2006 Tajikistan had the highest infant mortality in Central Asia, with 56 deaths per 1,000 live births. For the same year, Kazakhstan had the lowest infant mortality rate of 26 deaths per 1,000 live births.)

Much later, our room became a go-between from another bedroom wherein slept two Swiss gentlemen. The Dutch and Swiss had had a bit of a party (why didn't we crash it?) with much drinking and story-telling. We got safely to bed with no interruptions, but then it started. The Swiss stumbled noisily and drunkenly in and out all night en route – we presumed – to the toilet, waking us each time they bumped into things. They knocked over furniture, and generally behaved as some folk do after an evening's imbibing. We could afford to feel very self-righteous.

All was forgiven the next morning as we had a very jolly breakfast altogether, sharing our jams and glutting on *kaimak*. Altyn must have asked the Dutch if they had any spare vodka, for, just as we were about to leave, one of the young men proffered a barely started bottle of vodka for us, refusing my offer of payament. What a generous gesture. He would be able to replace it later that day in Osh. I was so thrilled I flung my arms round him giving him a big thank-you kiss. God, I sound like a real old dipso! As we were bidding everyone goodbye, Hettie asked us why we were doing this trip in Tajikistan. "Curiosity," we responded. "We are both interested in how other people live."

"Well," she responded, "my parents wouldn't dream of coming here, they wouldn't sleep on the floor or cope with the food, and as for the toilets... well, it would be out of the question. At your age, and I don't want to be rude, but I think it takes a very special sort of person to cope with it all." It was so complimentary of her. We don't really think we are doing anything particularly special, but nevertheless, we felt quite proud at her kind words.

Jalang and the Snow Leopard.

Heading south, a few miles from Karakul, the track branched off the Pamir Highway to the right. In the early morning light, the lake looked a different fantastic colour to the day before, like a giant glittering mirror, reflecting the deep blue sky. We were giving a lift to a little girl, the daughter of the yurt family at Jalang where we would spend the night. Our track bent round the southern end of Lake Karakul through an icy river and across a wide, shallow, desert valley. Here we entered The Pamir National Park, with the highest of the Pamirs all around us. It was so barren, just stony desert without a blade of vegetation. I noticed an ominous, spasmodic clicking noise coming from the front of the car. Pretending it wasn't happening and ignoring it, I kept my mouth closed hoping it wasn't too serious. The valley gradually became narrower as we proceeded upwards, with some yaks grazing the sparse grass beside the river which we crossed and re-crossed.

We passed one homestead of a yurt and animal enclosures, then, towards the end of the long narrow valley, Altyn pointed out our destination for the night. This had to be, without a shadow of a doubt the highest, most barren, most remote place we had ever been to, let alone slept in! This was what we had hoped to do years before when we were a little younger, in Kyrgistan. Then, instead of two nights yurt stay we were taken to Lake Issyk Kul and a quite different town of Karakol – a far cry from what we were now facing.

The two men who greeted us at the side of the track had sun-darkened faces. They embraced our boys warmly, obviously old friends. They were dressed in layers of clothes and woolly hats – it was going to be cold. The little girl who travelled with us hopped out of the car to be hugged by her mother, father and granny. This family is Kyrgis as are most of the population of eastern Tajikistan. Rather handsome but quite different to the Tajiks of the west. The men wore western clothes, but the woman wore the traditional long skirt and a woven yak-wool jacket, topped by a headscarf. Yet again pulling our boots off, we were ushered into the yurt, as ever, warm and cosy from the yak-pat-fuelled fire. We were given tea, bread and kaimak and assumed it was our lunch. The yurt was again beautifully decorated with bright hand-embroidered cushions and hand woven covers for mattresses. There was a screen, behind which were kept pots and pans. I went to examine the screen to find it was made of reeds. Each reed was separately bound in coloured wools, combining reds, blues and white. The reeds were then sewn together to form the screen, and the covered reeds, when joined together, revealed the beautiful design. How the operator knew when to finish one colour and start another I cannot imagine but it was a wonderful work of art. When I asked I was told it was about 50 years old, made by our hostess's grandparents – they are still made today.

Before long the boys got down to fixing the car, taking a front wheel off and revealing a cracked spring – no wonder. As they were fully occupied we took ourselves off to explore the valley with directions to where we should find some more petroglyphs. We dandered off up the river bank, chatting away. Elise suddenly went very quiet and excitedly nudged my arm and pointed down to the sandy bank. "Look, look," she whispered. "Isn't that a big-cat paw mark?"

We stood, frozen to the spot, looking around us, almost expecting an animal to be lurking somewhere near. We wondered could the marks be possibly from a snow leopard, or could we have mistaken them for just a large dog.

Official figures estimate anywhere between 120-300 cats in Tajikistan but although protected, they are still poached due to lack of funding and staff. Altyn told us he had often seen snow leopards around Murghab. We continued on uphill to find the enormous stone with the petroglyphs, a good two hour uphill trek. We stood around taking photos while a light blizzard drifted towards us. The sun was behind a peak, but the tiny ice crystals sparkled, back-lit, as they danced through the still air. It was quite entrancing.

Returning to the yurt we passed a lady coming towards us. I happened to turn to see where she was going. Not too far, and she whipped up her skirts, and hunkered down hidden by a mound of pebbles. She was so quick, I wondered if maybe they don't wear knickers here. Not surprising they don't go too far, the long-drop was a roofless stone enclosure a good walk uphill from the yurts.

In one of the other yurts a lady was sitting astride a piece of weaving which she was working at. About a foot wide, a black and red design, it was already a good few metres long. Slow and tedious, we watched her working away, changing the colours at every row. Using a traditional design, she was weaving the long band that goes round the top of the trellis that forms the collapsible wall of the yurt.

There was an enormous bull yak out on the pasture, very interested indeed in a small tethered cow with calf. He was grey and hairy with the long full tail of the yak family and two strange tufts of hair sprouting from the sides of his upper belly. He stood close, licking his lady-love's sides and nuzzling her neck and shoulders, much more amorous than she was. She would turn away seeming very half-hearted about his approach, maybe because he hadn't as yet produced a penis, or maybe she was shy and waiting for the privacy of the dark. We waited for ages watching to see what would happen. By 6.30 pm we were in the shadow of the mountains and although the wind had dropped it was cold. In the meantime the rest of the yaks had arrived down from the high pasture and were being milked by six of the ladies. After they had finished that little chore, they busied themselves shovelling up the dry yak pats and piling them up onto the already large mound. God, what a hard existence. And where were the men? We were told that they had *all* gone to get the lorry that will transport everybody and the folded up yurts, any day now, to Karakol for the winter. I do hope that what we pay these people will be fairly divvied out, including the women.

Surprisingly, we had spaghetti and the most delicious potatoes with *kaimak* for supper. Such a welcome change from the endless stew concoction, which wouldn't be so bad if it didn't have half an inch of sheep fat floating on top. Both of us have lost weight, partly from lack of hunger and partly by not being enticed by the food. Dogs were continuously barking outside. Often the yaks are attacked by wolves or snow leopards but the dogs are fierce enough to keep them at bay. I went outside and walked a distance up the hill at the back of the yurt. The darkness was absolute except for the magic of the stars. With no other light for miles around, I had never seen stars like it. They were breathtaking. The Milky Way streamed over my head like a wide bright road, while a myriad of glittering celestial bodies, although millions, or even trillions of light years away – unimaginable distances – seemed only just beyond my reach. Back inside, and again the evening hung heavily. Sitting on the floor was hard unless one could find something to lean against and although many of the yurts now have solar panels, the light provided by them is minimal and reading and writing is a bit of a struggle by torchlight.

In fact, everything was hard. Getting up from sitting made one's heart thump. It was all uncomfortable and we were way, way out of our comfort zone. I think also we were both tired. Packing and re-packing every day, un-rolling our mattresses and sleeping bags, and the unaccustomed altitude. But perhaps the hardest thing of all was the slight anxiety of not causing offence to our hosts by our inadvertent inappropriate behaviour. Our lovely hostess came in to make up our beds around 9.30, bringing us hot water to wash and making sure the stove was well-fuelled with yak dung. She was so caring for our welfare that we both had a little cry. Getting ready for bed seemed to be a marathon, but eventually, washed and warm, sliding into my sleeping bag, even on the floor, was pure bliss.

I lay on my back the following morning, awake early as usual, aware when the lady came into the yurt to stoke up the fire. I lay on, warm and relaxed, watching through the curved beams of the roof, as the white smoke curled up out of the chimney-pipe and into the clear blue sky. Dressed and outside in the sparkling clear air, our spirits rose along with the sun. Each day brought a new adventure of one sort or another; exciting and interesting. It was only in the evenings that our spirits flagged.

The Bartang Valley

The road from Jalang down the Bartang Valley where we were headed was, to say the least, a track into one of the most remote parts of Tajikistan. Neither the Lonely Planet, nor Odyssey's Companion and Guide to Tajikistan (both very different and both excellent guides) make any attempt to describe this area. You couldn't unless you had experienced it! Some of the alternative tour planners had warned us against taking this route as being too dangerous for a host of differing reasons. Did we heed them? No. The Tajik travel firm we eventually chose, and our boys, seemed to think it would be OK, and so we would soon find out. We only discovered later that nobody from the travel firm had ever been this way. Altynbek had only been once – on horseback. Asylbek, our driver – never.

Around 50 km/31 mi down the Kok Ubel Valley, we stopped, with relief, at the geometric symbols at Shurali. This is a most stunning archaeological ensemble of 15 geoglyphs spread out over the flat valley, probably between the 8th and 3rd centuries BC. Our track, for that is all it was, at times clung to the side of the mountain, at times running along the valley floor. Remote, it certainly is. I was perfectly camouflaged in our surroundings, wearing beige trousers and a grey T-shirt.

Our track hung an abrupt left turn at Kok Jar Pass where the Tanimas River flows east from a series of huge glaciers. The largest of these glaciers being the Fedchenko, at over 70 km/43 mi, **is** one of the world's longest. Here, we were stopped by a man and his family outside not much more than a hovel, at the side of the road. He asked for a lift down the valley. For reasons that they did not divulge, our boys refused him, saying it wasn't a good idea. I felt rather mean about it, but presumed they had their reasons. But how, I wondered, could any of them get to anywhere? With so little passing traffic, it would have to be a long trek on foot.

The single track, now running parallel to the raging Tanimas River was terrifying. A couple of thousand feet or more above the tree-lined river, with a sheer drop. I found myself practically on Altyn's knee beside me, in my effort to lean away from the track's edge. Elise, bravely, sitting in the front beside Asyl. Crikey, crikey! The mountain wall on our left hand side consisted of pebbles – beige, grey and red held tenuously together by dry, dusty clay. The lack of sunshine added to the austere landscape. All colour was drained from the sky, its low greyness becoming one with the land, the mountain contours across the valley blurred and indistinct. This was the most scary drive I have ever experienced – bar none. The Karakorum Highway was frightening, but there were plenty of people travelling along it – here we were solitary. No damn wonder we were advised against coming here.

Thankfully we had to stop, as the car, again, had a problem, so Elise and I elected to walk for a while down the track, while the boys attended to our vehicle. It had now become so windy that the dust swirled around us, blocking out our view across the valley, getting in our hair and covering my diary in grit. Here and there the sides of the track had broken away, tumbling down the mountain-side in mini-avalanches, leaving ragged edges to catch out the unwary motorist. If we had met another vehicle up here, I have no idea how we would have negotiated passing each other. With slow progress, we continued on. Using nerves of steel, Asyl negotiated the track. Sometimes we got out to walk when *our* nerves deserted us.

A few hours later we were able to relax for a while when we arrived at the village of Ghudara, a tiny village nestling in a small cultivated valley, walled-in by enormous mountains. We received a huge welcome from everyone we met. Here the Kok Ubel river reappears and joins the Tanimas, forming the Ghudara River. It looked as though almost everyone in the village was involved with harvesting the wheat. Groups of women and girls armed with hooks, slashed at the golden crop. With each swathe, they would, time consumingly, pick out every separate stalk of wheat, putting aside any greenery as fodder for the yaks. The wheat was short but fat and ripe. We were entertained to lunch by a couple of delightful girls and the keeper of the local hostelry, the dark-eyed Bobi. Wearing a scarf round his neck he told us he was sick. We were not sure what with. Of course, they weren't expecting us but were able to provide a veritable feast of potatoes, eggs and home grown, milled and baked brown bread. Along with some of our tomatoes, and washed down with the ubiquitus green tea, it was delicious. Somehow, someone had given Bobi the Odyssey Guide to Tajikistan, and although he couldn't read it, he was inordinately proud of it. He asked me if he could have a tomato for his child. It was so little to ask that we left the rest of our tomatoes with them. Bobi told us that we were the only tourists that year and it was by then September so there wouldn't likely be any more. We explained, through Altyn, that we had been warned by various parties against coming to the Bartang Valley because of the state of the roads. He agreed that the road was terrible, but that the

Soviets had kept the road open, and in reasonable repair, thus enabling both the locals and visitors use the road safely.

We were sorry to leave such enthusiastic hospitality, but off we had to go to test our bravado against the perils of the road! We drove through one valley, which looked as though some giant had marched along scattering enormous rocks indiscriminately as though a handful of seeds. Later, we had to cross the river. Elise and I walked across with Altyn, searching for nails that sometimes pop up out of the planks and hammered them down with stones. The river, now that we were close to it, was grey with glacial silt and raging down the valley. It was perfectly obvious that bridges could so easily be swept away. At a quieter spot we passed a little farm with four donkeys tied together being driven round and round winnowing the wheat. Back again over the river and up and up a switch-back track. Huge lumps of slate were now perched above, ready to fall at any moment and flatten us. After the dull morning, the sun began to make a reappearance to welcome us to our homestay for the night at the village of Savnob.

We were now in a typical Pamiri house. We entered through a lobby with a raised dais. Through a small corridor used for washing and cooking and into the main room which comprised an open 'well' area in the middle surrounded by three raised platforms. Five supporting pillars symbolise the five members of Ali's family. In this house, an artist of some talent had painted a delightful, summery mural of local scenes in bright primary colours. We greeted our hosts with the familiar '*Salaam Alaykum*', left our bags, and went to explore.

After the cold wind earlier and having descended all day, it was good to feel a rise in the temperature. The first person we met was a man, either very drunk, very drugged or not quite the full shilling. He tried to talk and follow us but we made our way up to a ruined fort, now used as a toilet and managed to leave him behind. Another man was hard at work, winnowing grain with a flail. We watched as the chaff blew away up the valley on the strong breeze. Back across the road, we walked down to where the river was, metres below, at the bottom of an eerie black slate chasm. We continued our walk through small fields, followed by a donkey, when it began to rain heavily, curtailing our progress. Back in the B&B we thought, yet again, it was intended that we all sleep together. We weren't quite sure what was happening. Our boys were sitting or sleeping quietly on the platform beside us. Altyn was always unsure and didn't take the initiative about the sleeping situation which left us somewhat in limbo. There was enough electricity for a dim bulb and Elise wrote intently in her jotter – maybe she was writing a book! But I seemed to have come to a grinding halt. We were in a house in a village so far removed from home, that I felt confused and uncomfortable. The only sound was the sheet of plastic, covering the hole in the roof, flapping in the wind tearing through the valley. I would just have to wait and see what would happen later on.

I was up before the sun at 7 am. We were in such a deep valley that the sun was just touching the highest peaks around us but didn't appear until a little before 9 am. Happily, we had had the room to ourselves after all last night. Cocks were crowing and Elise came out to join me watching a neighbour chasing her three goats up the hillside for the day's grazing. The sons of the house did some odd chores before school. Behind the house, the golden pile of grain lay still before the man with the flail returned to finish his winnowing. We stood quietly, watching the village coming to life, when, down the field below us, we spied yesterday's donkey. It was galloping, pleasure-bent, chasing a female donkey up the field and along the village street, followed by its owner plus an enthusiastic crowd. We laughed so much that the others nearby, hearing our laughter joined in with us. Thank God, nobody seemed to take offence.

Another day of tortuous bends and death-defying drops. Downhill past a weather station, through a pebble valley, inching forwards over another bridge, then relaxing when we hit a smooth bit when Asyl enjoyed putting his foot down. All the time travelling through this crumpled crust of the earth. And there was I, thinking today it was all over and we would be tiddling along on the level – dream on Diana. We rounded a corner and saw on our left-hand side another small, very pretty, white village. We went flat out through Roshorv, over and through clear little rivers and tiny green and gold fields. Although Altyn had told us he had guided a posse of horsemen and women down the Bartang Valley, neither of the boys had ever been here before. Indeed, a bridge had been washed away, and we had had to take a detour. Roshorv is directly south of Revolution Peak and the jumping-off spot for the hard trek up to its 6,940 m/21,000 ft summit.

Another car was in front of us. Good Lord, what a surprise. It was the first to encounter a man on a donkey on the narrow road. The man hopped off his mount, and scurried to the edge of the road, dragging his donkey out of harm's way. Then we drove up and he had to do it again. He must have wondered what the world was coming to – two cars in one day!

We stopped by the side of a clear little stream running across the road into the Bartang River, and filled up our bottles with clean cold water, the surrounding vegetation bright with autumn colours. I thought, I could launch my little home-made coracle here. I would float down this Bartang River, into the Panj, then the Amu Darya and end up either in the Karakum Canal, a cotton plantation, or, with a lot of luck, the Aral Sea.

We kept coming across small land-slides. Nothing in comparison to the Karakorum Highway, but it had an army of maintanance workers always at the ready. Here it's 'do-it-yourself' as we soon discovered when we came upon six or so local men working on a more major fall. The car in front of us had stopped, disgorging four more helpers, then we stopped and Altyn, Elise and I started throwing some of the smaller rocks down the valley. It didn't take long to make the track passable again, but it's all *so* fragile. It only takes one good shower of rain to shift the loosly-packed stones creating an immediate landslide.

As we drove over another bridge at the entrance to the village of Basid, we saw two men messing about in a tributary river. We were stopping here anyway for lunch, so we got out and went to see what they were doing. They were turning over stones and catching water insects for fishing bait. We followed them as they baited fishing hooks with the insects, then patiently sat with rods, waiting for the catch of the day. Right enough, very soon, one man caught a smallish fish which he indicated was good to eat. I learned that '*riba*' is Tajik for fish. I think it's the only word I remember in Tajik – very useful. On the other side of the river, we watched a man approach a bridge, carrying an enormous bundle of grass on his back. Without hesitation he stepped onto and trotted across the precarious-looking rope bridge swinging in the wind and WITH NO SIDES to hold on to. We climbed up to the bridge with the thought of crossing it, but with the raging waters below and nothing to hold on to, we decided discretion was the better part of valour and funked it. This was a pretty village with lots of trees, ancient survivors of the severe climate.

Through another village, and we met up with some boys who turned up when we found ourselves in someone's potato patch. They advised us to turn again and cross another bridge as the track we were on petered out ahead (as far as I could see, it had already petered out).

It was mid afternoon when we arrived at the bridge which leads to the Geisev Valley. We had heard that the Geisev was very pretty with several lakes and good for trekking. The plan had been to arrive here during the morning, but with the detours, we had lost a lot of time. We left Asyl with the car – he deserved a snooze after all the dramatic driving he was having to do – and off we set. It was a great walk along a narrow track above the river. Then turning left into the mountains alongside a stream and uphill through trees, shrubs and wild lavender for about an hour until we arrived at the first lake. At this time of year the lake was quite small but we could see to where it had risen in the spring with the melt-water leaving a high watermark of branches and logs. There was a little glen of trees tightly tucked between the steep mountains. We would have loved to continue up to the next lake but the sun was already hidden behind the peaks and we had to call it a day.

By now, almost at the end of the Bartang Valley, we stayed the night in the village of Yents again in a traditional Pamiri house. We were greeted by an elderly couple who fussed over us making us comfortable with mattresses and cushions and plying us with the inevitable tea and sweets. The elderly lady kept shouting at us, trying to make us understand what she was saying by shouting. We realised she was trying to make us understand something, but of course the louder she shouted, the more I wanted to giggle. Eventually she went away and brought back some milk. I think she had wanted to know if we wanted milk, so the problem was solved. A young brother and sister came into the main room to do their school homework. Elise was great, helping them with their English which was really quite good. I gave them the rest of my post cards to take to school which delighted them. The children then took us outside to the little earthenware reservoir which they had replenished with hot water for washing. Fascinated, they watched our every move, as did Granny who terrified me – she never smiled. These grandparents were, for all intents and purposes, bringing up the children – five of them – as their parents were away in Moscow working. Tough for everybody. There is a small power station down-stream from Yents so we had slightly better lighting. In the late evening the eldest boy came in to pray. He knelt, palms upwards on his knees, facing towards Mecca, in an attitude of supplication he quietly chanted verses of the Koran.

We found the entire family, seven in all, sleeping in the ante-room when we went out in the morning, with our boys on divans in the garden. As usual, we felt guilty as we had the entire main room, depriving everyone of their normal sleeping area.

218

Back on the M45 and Civilization?

Gradually, as we drove west the valley broadened out and became green again with poplars and fruit trees. The road smoothed into tarmac as we hit the M45 at Rushan. Back again on the Pamir Highway with the terrors of the Bartang left behind we were able to relax. For all the terrors, there was also the exquisite remoteness, inhabited by people whose unbelievably hard lives have been shaped by their environment. Already it almost seemed to have been a dream – sometimes a nightmare, but one I wouldn't have missed for a fortune.

Again and again I wished we could take some of our acquisitive youngsters from the U.K and let them see how the other half lives.

Suddenly we were back in relative sophistication and were able to get petrol from a pump instead of jerry cans from the roof of the car. At least we hadn't had to use the tent also lashed on the roof in case of emergencies. We had only seen just the one other car all the days since we left Karakol. We had thought that this part of Tajikistan was tough enough, when we came by this way some weeks past. We hadn't even begun to discover what 'tough' really was. Back to the broad, flat valley and the Panj River where my coracle would take a breather after the rough and tumble of the Bartang and before the river narrowed again to a rocky river bed and a welter of white water. At a police stop we had to get out of the car while it was searched by two or three surly young policemen. The thorough search included scrabbling through our bags. What on earth, I wondered, could we be bringing *back* from the Pamirs? There was only one thing – drugs, of course. A tall young onlooker gazed expectantly at us, rubbing his naked belly up under his T-shirt. And then, suddenly, everyone was smiling with relief that we were not drug-running. So were we!

Having been a couple of nervous wrecks for several days, we thought the worst was all behind us by now. We were wrong. We were standing looking at the scenery when there was a scatter of

219

stones on the back of the car. Altyn shouted to us to get into the car as the rest was about to come down. To our horror, when we turned to see what was happening, we saw we had only just missed a rock fall! Earlier we had passed a bulldozer and a lot of broken-down lorries where there had been a previous avalanche.

Some of the international road signs kept me amused as we drove along. They were somewhat of an understatement. For instance… 'Steep Hill', 'Sharp Bend', 'Rock Fall', 'Curve', (there weren't many of those), 'Road Narrows', and the funniest of all, at a sign to beware of land mines of a man bending forward looking back over his shoulder at a little puff of smoke as though he had just farted.

We stayed again at our nice guesthouse in Kala-i-Khum where we sat up on the balcony enjoying the warm, humid evening and being waited upon by the charming Mirov. It seemed thundery and then as there was a flash of lightning, the electricity failed but we sat on eating Mrs Mirov's delicious plov in romantic candlelight. The local mullah's, now familiar '*Allah Akbar*' – God is Great – calling the faithful to prayer, mixed with the sound of the river was so evocative. But not for long. The gentle sounds were soon to be out-done by the short but fierce thunderstorm and accompanying torrential rain. Sheltered, we sat it out, relishing the almost forgotten smell of wet earth.

Having negotiated the hairpin bends up to the Khaburabot Pass in the wake of a train of Chinese lorries, we then faced the broken bridge again – down into and across the river. Then another road block, indicated by a line of stones across the road, where we had to blaze a trail across-country until we met the road again. Several times we saw wrecked ex-Soviet tanks in the river left there since the *Basmachi* uprising in 1922. Asyl was again so impatient, taking ridiculous risks, passing lorries on bends. I found I was gripping the handle of the door so tightly my knuckles hurt.

Shades of Old Soviet Times and 'The End'.

There had been so many hiccups on the road that by the time we got to Obigarm, Altyn suggested we stay there the night as it was already almost dusk. We arrived at an ex-Soviet sanatorium to get a non-greeting from the janitor. It was such a change to find someone so grumpy and unhelpful. Nevertheless he showed us to a room. Although it was en-suite it was grim. The toilet seat was filthy and the bucket for paper unemptied. Horrible. The place reminded us of the sanatorium we stayed in at Lake Issyk-Kul in Kyrgistan – at least it had a stunning view and was clean. This place also had a frig into which we put our fruit drinks. We asked to have the room cleaned while we went outside to have a look around. There were still flower gardens but everything was terribly over-grown and shabby. The fountains didn't work and it all reeked of a bygone era. We wondered if anyone else ever stayed here. As we walked around in the twilight, we were aware of a cacophony of bird song. Following the sound, we arrived at a derelict building into and out of which hundreds of birds were flying, doubtless going to roost. I wondered idly if there would be lots of fornicating going on during the night. Then in a few weeks time some poor little ravished bird would give birth to a clutch of eggs, not knowing who the father was.

We had all decided to eat out and the boys went off to suss out the eateries. There weren't any. So they brought back some bread and fruit, and we dined on our own noodles, chilled juice and a teaspoonful each of vodka, all that remained of the present from the Dutch guy. At breakfast the following morning, for the first time, we saw two fat people – the ladies at the table beside us. Before we left, the chambermaid stopped us in our tracks, wanting to search the room to ensure we hadn't pinched anything. What was there to pinch? I think poor Altyn was very embarrassed. After all the time we had spent in the High Pamirs with such lovely people, this was a really sad reflection of past times.

We were glad to leave the sanatorium and so, obviously, was the janitor. He happily waved us on our way smiling broadly. The road from Obigarm to Dushanbe was tarmac – with crash barriers and not so many 'dangerous bend' signs. I guess if you and your car have survived the vicissitudes of the High Pamirs until now, you deserve to get to Dushanbe in one piece.

The rain that had threatened all day fell heavily with accompanying thunder and lightning, just as we were getting ready to go out from our hotel back in Dushanbe. And then, suddenly, all the lights went out – everywhere in the city – everything – street-lights included. We had been invited out for dinner by Parvis Rakhimov the then owner of Somon Travel who had organized our trip. A Tajik, who normally lives in London with his family, by happy coincidence was visiting his parents while we were also in Tajikistan. We managed to finish dressing by torchlight (we thought we had left this little inconvenience behind) and traipsed down the stairs to where Parvis was waiting in the darkened foyer. He was totally charming as he guided us to his car. Of course the headlights worked, but I did wonder how we would negotiate the crossroads with no traffic lights. What odds, everyone just threw caution to the winds, taking their chances. We weren't going to get back to civilization that easily.

As it was the end of Ramadan and a holiday, Parvis said all the restaurants were shut so he was taking us to his parents' home. We didn't mind in the least – it's always more interesting going to people's homes. He introduced us to his pretty wife, his mother and of course, with huge pride to his young son. It was a delightful evening eating by candlelight, although faced with a table groaning with food. Delicacies of all kinds, and more kept appearing from the kitchen. Along with lots of recounting of our journey, we gave Parvis a few helpful hints for forthcoming travellers to the High Pamirs. We were amazed that Parvis had never been to eastern Tajikistan. We also learned that very few Tajiks from Dushanbe *ever* go east – AND – that we were his first clients to come to Tajikistan! He, in turn was amazed and quite incredulous that we should have wanted to go to such a difficult area at our age. "Aha," said Elise, "so you did see what age we were from our passports."

"I was horrified," he said, "and tried to find out about insurance in Tajikistan, but nobody would touch it."

Certainly, Parvis had phoned me to warn of the difficulties and discomforts of the homestays of the High Pamirs, but I had laughed it off and said we both had a fair idea what to expect. Squat toilets and sleeping and eating off the floor, and that if we didn't do it now – we just might never do it.

We had, indeed, and inadvertantly, saved the best – or worst – till last.

Independence Day, Ishkashim – dancer taking a call

Murghab. Wild east town

Pshart valley –
Gumbezkol, our host
with his Grandson

Spectacular Yamchun
Fortress – Wakhan
valley

AFTERWORDS

Unusually I didn't sleep a wink during the flight home from Tajikistan. This visit to Central Asia would probably be our final one and after a difficult horrible personal couple of years I was on a bit of a high. Something, I suppose, to do with the buzz I get from travelling and discovering a whole new world out there. Each day bringing a new experience makes me live a little. I also realize just how very lucky Elise and I are – still able to do this sort of travel and having each other to travel with. Sharing the ups and downs – the delights and discomforts – not to mention accommodation with the local people – were experiences not afforded to many.

I love it. I love the challenge. From my middle class, rather tame world, where amenities are always to hand – you flick a switch and, bingo, instant light... turn on a tap and you get, at the very least, clean, drinking water. It's all so easy and of course taken for granted and about a million miles from the everyday lives of so many of the people we have met in Central Asia. I feel triumphant in having survived no running water, the squat loos and lack of chairs and beds, and come out of it again enriched by the experience and learning a little bit about how the people of Central Asia live. And quite a lot about myself.

So what, in fact, have we two curious ladies learnt?

The countries of Central Asia are quite wonderfully diverse. They are different from one other particularly geographically. Steppe, mountain and desert, thus dictating the lifestyle of their inhabitants. Although they have always had fairly distinct cultural identities for centuries, these countries, having only become sovereign states since 1991, are still coming to terms with having to do without their dependency upon the Soviet Union. But they are nearly all quite wealthy in natural resources.

Kazakhstan – which of course we never managed to explore, is enormously rich in oil.

Turkmenistan's wealth lies in natural gas, and although the desert covers 80% of the land it is the world's 10th largest producer of cotton. Although the country lacks adequate export routes, the growth of Turkmenistan is apparently an amazing 16th in the world.

Uzbekistan is the world's seventh largest producer of gold and has significant quantities of natural gas, coal, copper, silver and uranium. However, although it is the world's second largest producer of cotton, many Western companies have boycotted the importation of cotton as it is produced by unpaid and child labour, (as we discovered for ourselves).

Kyrgistan is the second poorest country in Central Asia despite backing from the IMF, the World Bank and the Asian Development Bank. Kyrgistan's mountainous land is suitable for an agriculture-based economy, producing wool, meat and dairy products. The export of these commodities has been severely affected by the loss of the vast market in the Soviet Union after its break-up. Kyrgistan has substantial deposits of coal, gold and uranium. The country, is becoming a venue for climbing and eco-tourism.

Tajikistan is the poorest country in Central Asia. Its chief sources of income are aluminium production – having one of the largest plants in the world – and cotton growing. The Nurek Dam, currently the highest dam in the world, produces vast amounts of electricity. The export of electricity could bring in much needed revenue. With its fabulous scenery and delightful people, Tajikistan could also be a venue for eco-tourism but lacks many amenities.

All these Central Asian countries have a good adult literacy rate, in the high 80s and 90s% and as we found ourselves many people have some understanding of English.

Although everyone we talked to was proud of their independence but despite some of the appalling horrors of the early days of the Soviets, almost without exception, the man and lady-in-the-street that we were able to converse with, reckoned they had been better off under Moscow's wing. For so many years of the state being responsible, people are still finding it hard coming to terms with privatisation. Although, as time goes on young people have many more opportunities and seem to be making the most of their entrepreneurial skills.

There is still, however, a huge lack of jobs almost everywhere, leading to poverty and crime. Alcohol and drug addiction is rife. Indeed, close to one village that we visited, which shall be nameless, we found, in a large gloomy cleft in some rocks, an enormous cache of used hypodermic needles. Maybe thousands of them, certainly hundreds. It was an un-nerving discovery to find that someone, or many, had been using these.

There are still, of course, the ancient rhythms of life, but with satellite TV, the internet and tourism, almost everyone can discover how the rest of the world lives and what is available out there. Just how long, indeed, will villages like Damla in the Karakum desert of Turkmenistan exist?

So what would any traveller expect to find in Central Asia? In spite of the various problems, it is the most historically and culturally fascinating place I have ever been to. Turning back the clock to the days of the old Silk Road, with sumptuous ancient buildings and marvellous local markets in every town, all coming from a bygone age. And as for the areas of overwhelming physical beauty, with wild snow-capped mountains, huge glaciers, and tumbling rivers, what more could any visitor desire.

But most of all, for me, the attraction is in the people. The one uniting factor for the countries of Central Asia, is a gradual reversion to Islam. Hearing this might make anyone from the West take fright. But, no, on the contrary, rather than posing any kind of threat, one would find it is much more likely to represent immense kindness, friendliness, and an extraordinary and touchingly generous sense of hospitality.

And as for Elise and me? Well, we intend continuing our 'out-of-the-way' travels as long as we can. Or before the strictures of the airports of today totally confound us. Then, perhaps, we will spend some rather more gentle time exploring our own Emerald Isle.

FURTHER READING

Christine Du Fresne: Where Heaven and Earth Meet. A Journey Through Central Asia. In 1999, she went to Northern Kazakhstan. Her travels took her through NW China, Mongolia, Siberia, Kazakstan, Uzbekistan, Kyrgistan and N Pakistan. Published in Australia 2004. oop.

Isabella Bird: Born 1831. Journeys in Persia and Kurdistan. Pub 1891

Dervla Murphy: Where the Indus is Young. Author travelled with her young daughter up through Pakistan and the Karakorums to Baltistan. Pub 1977

Ella Maillart: Turkestan Solo. A Journey through Cenral Asia. In 1932, the author travelled from Moscow to Kyrgistan, over the Tien Shan mountains and into the Taklamakan Desert. She saw Samarkand, Bukara and Khive. A remarkable story.

Jill Worrall: A Blond in the Bazaar. Author's adventures in Pakistan. Pub 2003

Georgie Anne Geyer: Waiting for Winter to End. An extraordinary journey through Soviet Central Asia. The author's experiences in Kazakstan, Kyrgistan, Uzbekistan, Tatarstan and Azerbaijan. Pub USA 1994

Lady Catherine Macartney: An English Lady in Chinese Turkestan. In 1898, Sir George and Lady Macartney travelled to Kashgar where they lived for many years while he was British

Consul there. A great insight into travel in the late 1800's. First pub 1931

Nick Danziger: Danziger's Travels. Pub. 1993. Central Asia and Tibet, meeting mullahs, lamas, and all sorts of characters.

Eric Newby: A Short Walk in the Hindu Kush. Newby and friend, Hugh Carless travel from Mayfair to Afghanistan to climb the mountains of Mir Samir. Pub. 1958

Geoffrey Moorhouse: Apples in the Snow. A Journey to Samarkand. Pub 1990

Giles Whittell: Extreme Continental Blowing Hot and Cold Through Central Asia. Journey round Central Asia by motorbike. Pub 1995

Colin Thubron: Shadow of the Silk Road. Author travels across China, Afghanistan, Iran and Turkey. Pub 2007

Colin Thubron: Lost Heart of Asia. Author's depressing journey through part of Central Asia. Pub 1994

Peter Hopkirk: Foreign Devils on the Silk Road. Historical. Search for lost cities and treasures in Chinese Central Asia. Pub 1984

Peter Hopkirk: The Great Game. The struggle for Empire in Central Asia circa late 1800's. Pub 1991

Peter Hopkirk: Setting the East Ablaze. Lenin's dream of an empire in Central Asia. Pub 1995

William Dalrymple: In Xanadu. In 1986, the author travels across Central to Xanadu in Mongolia, following the journey of Marco Polo. Pub 1999

Jonny Bealby: Silk Dream – Troubled Road. Horseback through Central Asia. Pub 2003

Sven Hedin: The Silk Road. 10,000 miles through Central Asia. First pub 1938

Sven Hedin: The Trail of War. Author's expedition to Xinjiang Province of W. China in 1930's. New edition pub 2008

Greg Mortenson and David Oliver Relin: Three Cups of Tea. One Man's Mission to Promote Peace…One School at a Time. Mortenson's inspirational story of bringing schools to Baltistan in northern Pakistan. Pub 2006

Lutz Kleveman: The New Great Game. Blood and Oil in Central Asia. Pub USA 2003

Wilfred Blunt: Golden Road to Samarkand. Pub 1973

Daniel Metcalfe: Out of Steppe. The Lost Peoples of Central Asia. A Central Asia far removed from the home of "Borat" the Kazak. Pub USA 2009